The Depths of I

Eliminating Indifference

Joe Robert Thornton

VIZZIONNARY
PUBLISHING   BRANDS

The Contents

"The opposite of excellence is not failure-
it is something worse... mediocrity."

~ Joe Robert Thornton

"There is another condition just as destructive
as mediocrity... indifference."

~ Joe Robert Thornton

This book is dedicated to my children-
Christian, Nymera, and Ryan. The Loves of my life.

From The Author

I recognize that it is uncommon for an author to provide remarks in the foreword of their own book; however, I want to share insight on why I have one of my children, Christian, writing the introduction to this book.

Christian is the last born of our three children. Depending on who you ask, the last child gets everything, or they get the leftovers from their siblings. As a father, I hope the answer is neither, as my wife and I always worked hard to demonstrate fairness amongst all three children. We have also realized that every child is different, and they each need something different.

With Christian, we almost lost him years ago as he had given up and attempted to end his life. Unfortunately, my wife had to experience Christian going through this attempted suicide up close and personal. Ultimately, there is a happy conclusion to this part of his story. Christian pulled through... and that is all that matters to us.

We are so proud of the young man that he has become. When I

thought about mediocrity and indifference for the topics of this book, I thought about Christian's renewed approach to life.

Christian is exceptionally determined. When he decides that he is going to do something, he is all in with maximum effort.

Christian's commitment to pursuing anything in his life is inspiring... and an inspiration for me to write about mediocrity and indifference. If everyone had Christian's dedication to excellence, there would be little mediocrity and indifference in the world.

Based on Christian's passion and purpose-driven thinking, his words have special meaning to me and particular relevance to the content of this book.

Foreword

I used to assume that having an impenetrable focus was the key to becoming successful. However, if you only operate with one goal or focus, you limit yourself from other life experiences. These experiences will aid you in becoming successful too. But you must let them in. I firmly believe that the only possible way to manifest your full potential is by experiencing as much as you can.

Not only that, you must get comfortable with failure. Humans naturally adapt by trial and error. As I have heard others say before me, failure is something that builds character.

I recognized at an early age that commitments need to be great, or those commitments will not count for anything. So, if I am going to fail, I would rather fail with a valiant effort.

So, what can we do to ensure that success indeed happens? The answer is...

Sacrifice.

At 25 years of age, I have sacrificed years upon years chasing my dreams. Although I have had my share of fun, I have spent much more time building my legacy, which is a lonely road but worth it in the long haul.

I have poured my soul into everything I have attempted to do. Whether playing soccer, writing hundreds of songs, producing music, starting a record label, pursuing a mixed martial arts career, or helping others as a certified fitness trainer... it is all about passion. Passion does not allow for mediocrity or indifference.

And that is what brings me to this discussion about my father. My father is 56 years old. Yet, in my mind, he is 56 years young, with such an untouchable drive. It is a drive so strong that it cannot wither away no matter the dark stormy days he has experienced or the lonely roads he has traveled.

Another amazing point. My dad still plays basketball. Even after breaking his arm three times- twice in the last four years, he still plays. This does not include the ACL surgery he had on his knee a while back. Overall, I am blown away by his physical and mental ability to push forward and focus so precisely.

My dad has continued to work at a high level, personally and professionally- all his own will. He manages to make it look easy all the time. But I know that is because of his preparation and desire. Like my father, I believe that everything must be done the right way.

However, this does not mean that my father excels at everything.

Of course, everybody has their weaknesses. I find he is human, just like the rest of us, even when he has convinced us otherwise. It is pretty funny that growing up, we always used to call him Superman or Super Dad. Mostly because he constantly did what no father could do- show us love while working at such a mechanical pace.

My father is a real-life example of success. Yes, he has made mistakes, and he has regrets as everyone else does. However, the difference between my father and everyone else is that he has made the appropriate sacrifice to turn failure into success.

This supports his position of not accepting mediocrity or indifference. No one is perfect, but that does not mean we cannot pursue perfection. I pursue it, my dad pursues it, and I believe that brings out the best in all of us.

My father is not indifferent either. On the contrary, he always has a position... on everything. He is a very independent thinker-other people will not influence him by what they say or believe.

I understand why writing about mediocrity and indifference is essential to him. My father cares deeply about the world around him and is affected by everything happening in our environment today.

This book is not about getting everyone to live as my father lives; it is about getting everyone to live to their highest capabilities.

My dad's hope and mission are for this book to help you unlock something in your thought process that will point you toward more purpose and more passion, less mediocrity, and less indifference.

A warning, though, this is not a feel-good book. Instead, this is a book to make you feel what you need to feel. In other words, it will take you out of your comfort zone- hopefully enough to compel you to act.

These two words- mediocrity and indifference have become a referendum for my father regarding how he lives. He believes that allowing either of those to exist makes a statement about who we are.

My dad, Joe Robert Thornton, is imploring us to look at all aspects of the world around us through the lens of mediocrity and indifference... and the consequences of each.

Finally, I believe this book will take you on a journey to help you examine yourself thoroughly and help you discover how and what you could sacrifice daily to achieve greatness.

~ Christian Thornton

Preface

Let me start with this: this is not your conventional leadership book, although it does contain components of leadership: inspiration, vision, action, and results. I injected a little bit of hope as well.

However, as Christian shared, this is not a feel-good book. The intention of the book is to spark action. Sure, I hope that the stories entertain you and perhaps you find application of the leadership principles, but I also hope emotions are stirred inside of you.

There is a bit of a stream of consciousness throughout the book. There will be an intentional link from one chapter to another, but only to a point. From there, each chapter stands on its own.

I will describe this as a self-reflection book, not a self-help book. I am not sure how much my life experiences will help you, but if my perspective creates a moment of self-reflection in your own life, then I will feel that I have accomplished my objective.

I am not going to avoid conversations on important topics. At book's end, I hope you will be inspired, but I will be more satisfied if you are compelled to act.

In part because I feel that it is time for a reality check. As a society, I believe we are careening toward mediocrity and indifference at an alarming rate. I have seen mediocrity and indifference accelerating in leaders of all levels, and frankly, I have had enough. "Looking the other way," "taking the high road," and "waiting for this to pass" are just not getting it done. It is time to step forward and call out mediocrity and indifference whenever and wherever we see it.

I would love to tell you that I am saying this for dramatic effect to stimulate you as a reader, but I am not- there are real-life situations where the stakes of our daily lives are increasing with deadly consequences. Our collective freefall has been well-documented over the past few years... and topped off by the compounding effect of the recent global pandemic.

So, on that ominous note, I begin...

Average. So-so. Plain. Middle-of-the-road. All markers of mediocrity.

Unconcerned. Apathetic. Careless. Negligent. All markers of indifference.

Mediocrity and indifference are not words that we often use in everyday conversation. And that is precisely why I am calling them out in the title of this book.

Years ago, I spent time with a leader, Howard, who consistently used the word mediocrity, but when he used it, it was contextually condescending. He intended to motivate others, but the impact always seemed to land on the negative side. Howard would use it to describe the current state of the business, and while he was never talking about one individual, it always felt personally directed, nonetheless.

Mediocrity was a word that evoked a feeling of being inadequate, but it also made you feel compelled to take the hill, to do something about a situation. It is odd to have a word strike both disappointment and inspiration simultaneously. But again, on countless occasions with Howard, it most often landed on the side of disappointment.

The mere representation of being described as mediocre was offensive, and that emotion would be visible on the faces of the group members that Howard would address. Calling the group substandard would have been better. There was just something about the word mediocrity. Howard was achieving his objective. I swore there were times when he held back a smirk as he admonished the team. Howard's poor leadership impact and all, in part, inspired this book. Go figure.

Because of the word's resonance, I felt I needed to intentionally use the word mediocrity in the title. I often gravitate to words that evoke emotion, words that make you take notice. In my previous book, "The Hostility Of Change: Breaking Through Deep-Seated Barriers," it was right there in the title. Being hostile often has a precise meaning, often associated with anger- you can visualize someone being aggressive and the actions that would be demonstrated. Deep-seated has an emotion attached to it too-someone who will not move off a view due to a belief that is so deeply embedded that contrary information, or even facts, will not sway their opinion.

My intention with every book is to give you something you can take with you and to do so through storytelling, so this book is not just about describing mediocrity and indifference. The practical way each shows up and impacts our lives will also be explored. This book also veers away from a traditional leadership principled approach and into more present-day topics that have given rise to mediocrity and indifference.

Principles, theories, and concepts are important, but frankly, each of them can be boring. On the other hand, storytelling captures the imagination, so my hope for this book is to deliver compelling stories that inspire.

Let me linger on storytelling for a moment.

Storytelling is critical to getting points across in a way that is relatable to anyone needing to hear a key message. I believe that every life experience has a relatable story. I will be very intentional in this book about stopping to tell stories. So, if it feels like I am digressing, it is because I am. Here is digression number one:

I recall a conversation with a group of regional vice presidents I had worked with for many years earlier in my career. I was about to take on a new and broader role. So, I asked them what advice they would offer me for the new position. The collective response was simple- continue to tell stories on a larger scale. The group felt like stories I shared over the years helped them feel connected to others and inspired them to achieve more. I have always remembered that conversation and vowed to continue to tell stories on my leadership journey.

Back to the topic at hand.

Mediocrity and indifference are not the same; therefore, I am compelled to call them out separately in the title and subtitle. However, as it relates to the literal definition of mediocrity and indifference, there are similarities to call out:

The definition of mediocrity is not very flattering:

1. mediocrity (n.) being of no special quality or type: average, common, commonplace, cut-and-dried, formulaic, garden-variety, ordinary, plain, routine, run-of-the-mill, standard, stock, undistinguished, unexceptional, unremarkable. 2. Of low or lower quality: inferior, low-grade, mean, second-class, second-rate, shabby, substandard.

The definition of indifference is not so endearing either:

1: indifference (n.) the trait of lacking enthusiasm for or interest in things generally; Synonyms: apathy/numbness/spiritless. 2: absence of compulsion to or toward one thing or another: lack of difference or distinction between two or more things.

While both words evoke similar sentiments, the place where I do see the comparisons fall apart is how they manifest themselves. I believe that mediocrity is more of the tangible outcome, often from a feeling of indifference, while indifference is the feeling itself.

Now, Merriam-Webster and others may take exception to my oversimplification of definitions here, but I like to make things as easy to understand as possible in my writings. Well, except for the fact that I use big words, I do stick to pretty simple principles.

Again, with mediocrity and indifference, I recognize that these are not words we often use in everyday conversations and yet, each of them often show up in our daily lives.

I will say this: I do not believe anyone strives to be mediocre or indifferent. I am a Theory Y person- the assumption that people are internally motivated and work to improve themselves without needing a direct reward.

Mediocrity often denotes inadequate performance or pure inability... even with a Theory Y mindset.

However, multiple factors can cause mediocrity:

When it comes to substandard results in business, there are times when the issue, the gap, is even more concerning- the hard-to-detect apathetic leadership: the do-just-enough-to-get-by leadership.

I believe strongly in the following principle: Doing nothing or wishing a problem away is a form of poor leadership. Playing it safe has never shown up as a strong leadership strategy. Staying silent is not a good look, either.

The time has come for these shortcomings to be addressed.

Before discussing the book's title and subtitle, I want to discuss the front cover image.

Many of you have probably heard the term "rolling the dice." This phrase originated sometime after the creation of gambling using a six-sided pair of dice. "Rolling the dice" became used in everyday life to describe taking a chance or a risk to get something worthwhile.

I chose this image because so much of our day-to-day life is about the decisions we make and the risks we take. We are rolling the dice with every decision. Our choices have consequences.

This point about "rolling the dice" is not about challenging decision-making, only acknowledging that every decision comes with some risk. The relevant point here is that if we are not conscious of every decision, we can get careless, lose discipline, become indifferent, and fall into mediocrity.

I understand that may sound negative, but this is real-life stuff. So often, it is not the one big thing that knocks us off the track-it is a series of small things that add up.

Now, many of our day-to-day decisions may seem insignificant.

Still, in the end, most decisions have a cumulative impact on aspects of our life, like health or personal relationships.

So, the dice are a metaphor for all our decisions that can lead to many possible outcomes- the life decisions leading to either excellence or mediocrity, intentionality or indifference.

To go further, every dice added to the equation increases the possibilities thousands of times. So, I decided to show six dice in this picture to represent the intersection of six critical aspects of our lives- health, relationships, work, money, family, and friends. This intersection creates almost incalculable possibilities. For example, a poor money decision can negatively impact a relationship, or a new friendship could positively impact your health, and so on. Of course, there are many more aspects of our lives that I could represent here, but these six are relatable to most of us.

These dice represent the endless possibilities of rolling all six dice simultaneously and the unpredictability of our lives. The probability of rolling the same number on all six dice simultaneously is in the tens of thousands... and that is just the outcome of one combination.

Now, you may be wondering if this is relevant since most decisions in life may only have a couple of potential outcomes. Of course, that is fundamentally true, but when you recognize the threading of one decision in life to another, and the subsequent result, the possibilities begin to extrapolate fast.

Another aspect of this picture is that I intentionally chose wooden dice to reflect the story. There is a bit of an old-world, worn feel to anything wooden. The metaphorical context here is that our decisions may be made with worn-out or outdated beliefs. It is easy to get into a routine of day-to-day life and make mediocre decisions- decisions that are an automatic response without the proper investment of time or curiosity to find a potentially better solution.

Finally, the wooden dice also show the distress of wood, the imperfections, if you will. That is undoubtedly relatable to who we are as human beings- our flaws are often on full display. The decisions that we make are sometimes flawed too- made irrationally or made without complete or accurate information.

Let me shift gears and talk about the book title.

The title, "The Depths Of Mediocrity," is precisely what it implies- I believe there are performance levels on the way to mediocrity. I will explore examples of mediocre behaviors that result in egregiously poor leadership.

The title also implies that there are depths of behaviors, some more abhorrent than others, which point toward activity that crosses the line, at times legally and just as concerning, morally.

To contradict an earlier point about Theory Y people, some people may actually set out to be mediocre. For those people, being the best is not a priority. You know it when you hear a statement like, "No sense overexerting myself on something that may not be worth it or that I cannot attain."

I have heard that many times before. And it usually comes from the same person whining or complaining about the promotion at work they were expecting to receive but got passed over. All I will say is that most things in life are connected. If you do not care enough to try harder, you get what you get.

For clarity, this is a self-reflection book, not a self-help book. If I give it to you easy, nothing will change. However, if I give it to you straight, the probability of you doing something different may increase.

Mediocrity hits a nerve for me. I can say that after working with hundreds of leaders over the years, I could list many of them who were just mediocre. The journey for me has been to better understand why.

Earlier in the preface I mentioned that mediocrity often denotes inadequate performance or pure inability. I also mentioned that multiple factors can cause mediocrity. Let me expand on that more:

Some situations occur in our personal life that can impact our professional life, and vice versa, and that can cause us to become mediocre at what we are doing. It does not always mean that we stop caring; it may simply mean that we cannot invest the energy we once did due to current life circumstances. Sometimes it happens slowly, and we do not identify the change- i.e., the onset of a health condition that takes months or years to identify and diagnose. Other times, situations happen suddenly, and we recognize it but cannot prevent our slide to mediocrity- i.e., the death of someone close to us.

Of course, there is also the "Peter Principle"- getting promoted to a level of incompetence. There are times when our skills no longer keep pace with the new and elevated position that we find ourselves in, and thus, we become mediocre at what we do.

If we live long enough, there is a level of mediocrity that most of us will experience. It may not be intentional; it may not be avoidable; there is no malice; we simply fall into mediocrity with our work, school, relationships, etc.

I will not explore this type of mediocrity because we are all human beings and cannot reach perfection.

In this book, I want to address the obvious, intentional place we can arrive at with mediocrity by simply not exerting ourselves, not understanding the implications of this lack of effort, and not owning the deficiency when it occurs.

Let me pivot and share a bit about the subtitle, "Eliminating Indifference."

Indifference is a very troubling state of mind.

Indifference is far more damaging than your run-of-the-mill

poor effort. Indifference is not "I don't know what I am doing." Instead, it is "I know what to do and how to do it, but I simply do not care enough to do anything about it."

Indifference is so infuriating that it can turn something simple into something complicated. It shows up in small and big ways. For this book, I will focus on the significant impacts of indifference.

However, to provide context when discussing the significant ways that indifference can have a negative impact, I will take a moment to at least touch on a small way that indifference can creep into our lives: throwing a piece of paper at the trash can and missing, but not returning to pick it up.

I know what you are thinking- Joe, that is really small. But, of course, it is, and that is precisely the point. If you do not take care of the small stuff, I am not confident you will be inclined to address the big stuff.

Throwing trash out on the side of the street, putting a cigarette out and not throwing it away, not pushing your chair in at a table when you are leaving- I know, all small... but they matter.

If I were you, I would offer a counterpoint: Perhaps, what I am describing is not indifference; it is manners. Yes and no. Manners are the outcome- the often physical manifestation of someone not caring or being indifferent. The lack of care, the lack of emotion, and the lack of passion are what define indifference. Indifference then takes on a behavioral trait, such as walking by something that should require your attention, like trash on the ground before you — an important distinction.

Indifference, by actions, says that something is unimportant, not significant enough to care about it. This is a perfect example of why actions matter more than words. Someone could say they care about something but watch their actions. You know, the person who shows up fifteen minutes late for work every day, but you give them concert tickets to their favorite artist, and they show up an hour early. I am just saying... actions tell the story.

This book title and the book contents are intentional about linking mediocrity and indifference. The behavior of being indifferent usually spits out mediocre results, and any mediocre results are typically delivered by those who are apathetic about the quality of their work- personally or professionally. Mediocrity and indifference are often a packaged deal.

Ultimately, I prefer this book to be about hope and possibilities, so I will not linger only on the negative aspects of mediocrity or indifference. However, I must explore the dark side to get your attention.

This book is based on my own experiences, but I have also listened carefully to learn through other people's experiences and share their stories.

This book may make your head nod often; at least, I hope so. This book may also make you shake your head in disagreement, maybe even disgust, and I am good with that too. While positive affirmations are better, my intent is that this book will generate reactions that make you take stock of your own biases and, ultimately, take action to improve the world around you.

Justice, peace, kindness, joy, and happiness are under attack every day, primarily because of rampant mediocrity and indifference. I implore you to join the fight for good.

CHAPTER 1:

The Problem With Mediocrity

Let me begin with this quick story:

Years ago, I was listening to a professional football head coach give a speech to his team. His team was finishing a successful training camp and preseason schedule. The speech was incredibly inspiring- it had the making of something special. That was until the coach concluded the speech with this:

"This team has worked hard. Everyone on this team has laid it on the line for each other and demonstrated that we could play through adversity. I am proud of everyone on this team. In all my years of playing and coaching football, I have never been more excited about starting a new season."

"I need something more from each of you- I need your commitment to be your best on every play of every game. Then, I need you to go further. I believe that beyond your best is something better."

"It is time for us to show the rest of the league what we are made of. I do not believe there is a cap on the potential of this team. So now, let's go out and make the playoffs this year!"

Really? Make the playoffs? That is your big close? Let me explain why this is a problem:

The coach's statement unintentionally sows the seeds of mediocrity. It is a message to his team that the bar will be low enough that we can achieve satisfactory results and feel affirmed with our accomplishments. Sports, specifically, is a zero-sum environment- meaning, there will be as many losses as there are wins amongst all the teams when all is said and done with a game or a season, so someone ends up being mediocre or worse.

Proclaiming a successful season as defined by a playoff appearance is a problem because you could lose as many games as you win and still make the playoffs- it has happened on a few occasions.

What I am getting to here is the coach must set the bar higher if he expects a great result. This coach has set his team up to be good at best but, more likely, mediocre. Words matter.

I would submit that even a coach that gives the same passionate speech but concludes with the expectation of winning the Super Bowl has still left some opportunity on the table. The speech should arguably end with 'Let's win every game.' To achieve winning every game, the rest takes care of itself- you would make the playoffs and win the Super Bowl. Words matter.

I know you may think that what I am describing here is perfection.

However, even winning every game is not perfection- there are still missed tackles, dropped balls, fumbles, interceptions, and other mistakes on the way to winning every game. The coach should not allow the fear of perfection to stop his team from achieving the best result possible. Words matter.

In the end, the definition of perfection is, and arguably should be, a remarkably high and unattainable bar. By the way, if someone calls you a perfectionist, accept it as a compliment, even if there is intentional shade with their comments. Take it as them indirectly telling you your standards are higher than theirs.

The football coach, well-intentioned, lowered the bar before the season even began. I will challenge myself here- what if this team had lost every game the year before? Wouldn't making the playoffs be a huge accomplishment? To that, I say maybe. However, I view this as lowering the standard as well. If the team did go from a winless season to making the playoffs the following year, the coach could look back on the season and feel a level of satisfaction, but accepting a mediocre result before the season begins is rewarding improvement, not real change. Also, using the prior season as a gauge of success in the new season is a marker of mediocrity. It gives you an excuse if you do not have success in the new season. Basically, this can apply to any part of your life. Past mishaps should not drag down the expectation of a new moment.

Yes, I am beginning this book incredibly harsh. Mediocrity will find its way into your life unnoticed unless you root it out often and aggressively.

A business parallel here to the football example is leadership. The leader that pushes their team to be better, to be number one in their category, must still ask whether that is good enough. So, as a leader, are you planting the seeds of mediocrity with your team?

Understand that there is nothing wrong with being good at something, but do not confuse it with being great.

Think about the times you have said you are good at something. You are describing this in-between zone. Arguably, an average or median place.

I do not want to bring good down to the level of mediocre. However, good trending down toward mediocre differs from good trending up toward great. I will come back to this distinction shortly.

This is the perfect place to discuss great, good, mediocre, and poor results. In the preface, I referenced performance levels on the way to mediocrity. My interpretation is:

The first level of performance is Great.
Great is achieving best-in-class.

The second level of performance is Good.
Good is achieving, working for, or expecting better of yourself.

The third level of performance is Mediocre.
Mediocre is achieving inconsistently, blaming others for your performance, or criticizing others.

The fourth level of performance is Poor.
Poor is simply not achieving.

Let's explore each of these:

So, what is great? How do we achieve greatness? First, not everyone can achieve greatness. I know that sounds like a negative statement- it is not meant to be. Instead, it is the rationale that someone is on the top of the list- their competition, their profession. Someone is doing better than everyone else, much better. Great is indeed reserved for the few.

Think of it this way. If everyone was performing great, it simply means that the bar needs to be reset, and great is the new good. It takes leadership to recognize the difference between standout results and average results.

To be clear, great is the top-level, not the top quartile- great is more selective than that. If I were to quantify it, great is better characterized as, perhaps, the top ten percent.

So, what is good? Good is perhaps the most overused word when describing anything. Good is basically what it implies, and good is a wide range of performance. If I were to assign percentages here, good is about forty percent- the next forty percent below great. There is a caution here too.

Think about good here from a quantitative perspective. Take, for example, performance reviews- the bane of most progressive human resource professionals. Why? Because so many leaders, when given a five-point rating scale, will choose safely. Yes, the dreaded "three" rating. When this became a broad organizational issue years ago, some companies changed to a four-point scale. The result? Leaders still chose the "three" rating to avoid calling anyone a poor performer or being in the lower two quartiles. In effect, the four-point rating scale worsened the situation because leaders pushed average performers up in the overall rating process.

In more recent years, companies moved towards a three-point rating scale. Yes, that did help, as most people with a good rating mainly fell within the "two" rating. Unfortunately, for some companies, that did not get them to the finish line, so they solved the dilemma by eliminating performance reviews altogether. Well, I suppose that is one way to solve the problem. You may be noticing my sarcasm here. Solving a problem by eliminating the process should be carefully examined. Companies have run to do away with performance reviews because of the momentum behind the idea of it. All I will say here is, be careful.

I would not be surprised someday in the future to see performance reviews return in full force. In the end, either you give real performance feedback, or you don't. You can dress it up with cute new terms and use shorter forms, but in the end, you must stop and give performance feedback, if you want your people to grow.

Back to good performance- the point here is that there is a cautionary tale assessing good. Be aware of the possibility of overusing it.

Let me jump down to poor performance, and then I will come back to mediocre. Poor performance is the bottom ten percent, the opposite of great. There is always a bottom... the part no one ever wants to address. The question I often get is, "What if the bottom performers are performing too?" It is always interesting to watch people think about what they just asked now that they hear it aloud for the first time.

Nonetheless, I always get where they are going with the question. However, there is no team in the history of teams where everyone performs the same. There is always a bottom performer- the weakest link. I will get into this in more detail later in the book, but the bottom line is this:

If you accept the poor performers as good performers, you are widening your pool of mediocrity.

In addition, you are severely damaging your ability to have any material success, financial or otherwise.

Now that we have walked through great, good, and poor, I want to come back to mediocre.

Mediocre is the remaining forty percent... below good and above poor. I know what you are thinking, "Joe, why don't you just add a chart to your book to show the visual of the 100% of performance from great to poor?" It is a good question. But, of course, I do everything intentionally. As the reader, I want you to draw your own chart on paper. It is not quite kinesthetic learning, but interactive at least.

Mediocre performers are misdiagnosed more often than any other group. In part, it is because:

Mediocre is often disguised as good.

You will see many "bell curve" examples in business that talk about performance. One popular model talks about the top sixteen percent, the bottom sixteen percent, and the sixty-eight percent in the middle. Some models will show twenty percent at the top and bottom and sixty percent in the middle- you understand the correlative point here.

I believe the traditional bell curve example is flawed because it lumps too much in the middle. To be fair, that was not the intention of the creator of it. The creator seemed to have somewhat nefarious intentions for creating the bell curve- a topic for another time. Business leaders took the concept and adapted it for something else, but the point I am making tracks with this sizeable middle group of performers. The purported belief is that this large middle can be influenced to move up with the right motivation or inspiration.

Back to a point I made earlier in the chapter, good trending down toward mediocre differs from good trending up toward great. I believe that half of this mediocre group in the middle is pointed up toward good performance, and the other half is pointed down toward poor performance. To that point here, I would be careful. This middle percent is not created equal. More specifically, regarding the traditional bell curve example, half of the sixty-eight percent is likely performing well, and the other half is mediocre. This creates another potential examination- an active process to rank the middle within the middle.

The term "The Depths of Mediocrity" is about this level of performance that is exceedingly frustrating. We often excuse away poor performance and never get to diagnosing the problem. To that end, let's go deeper into analyzing mediocrity.

Mediocrity is everywhere. Let's face it, a lot has changed over the past twenty years in our world- we can get online and have anything delivered to our door in a matter of hours, we have thousands of channels and numerous streaming services available at our fingertips, and we can get answers to any question in a matter of seconds with the proper search engine or voice-assisted service.

However, I would submit that one thing that has not changed much over the years- mediocre leadership. While the world has moved at a fast pace, mediocre leaders and mediocre cultures have remained. Sure, we see entrepreneurs that have emerged to change the fabric of our daily lives, but that is a tiny group of people. Essentially, organizations nationwide still have ineffective, traditional, and uninspiring leaders. I know it sounds like gloom and doom... and that is because it is. Imagine what could be accomplished if all our leaders were great, or at least good, at what they do.

So, why are we still accepting mediocrity in this new age of business? Because most organizations and cultures are mediocre. Think of it this way- it is like a temperature setting in your house- if the thermostat is set to eighty degrees, when it gets warmer, the air conditioning kicks on to bring the temperature back down to its previous setting. This is what happens in organizational cultures every day. I contemplate this from an employee perspective:

If a courageous employee displays excellence or goes against the grain, the mediocre culture overtakes this one brave soul and brings them back to reality.

A high performer is no match for a culture of mediocrity. The result is that high performers often get fed up and leave, or sometimes even worse... they conform to the mediocre environment.

So, how do you spot this mediocre culture or identify if you are a part of one? Well, look for the signs. They are there... they are always there.

The first sign of a mediocre culture is that you may be hard-pressed to find the company's vision, mission, or values.

If this is your experience, run as fast as you can. Find another company to work for. I am being serious here. If the very foundation of what the company intends to stand for is not visible, there is no chance that the company is collectively behaving according to those expectations. On the other hand, if the vision, mission, and values are visible, then question whether people live them and believe in them. By the way, here is a hint:

If people in your organization cannot recite the vision, mission, and values, they are not living them.

You work in a mediocre culture if these steps are not in place. Plain and simple.

I will go a step further- even having the vision, mission, and values visible and living them is still not getting to the finish line. The additional confirmation of a culture intact is ensuring that all decisions are made through the lens of these beliefs. Best-in-class organizations will not allow any business decision to violate their cultural principles.

There is much more to cover here. What else? Behavior.

The collective behavior of everyone on the team determines culture.

When one person fractures the culture, it is fractured for everyone. This means that you must act when there is someone who behaves inconsistently within your culture. It would be best to get them out of your tribe as fast as you can. The reality is that the team already knows who will go against the grain of the culture, so it is usually not that big of a surprise when the poor behavior happens.

Another notch on the behavior conversation is this:

The culture is determined by the worst behavior leaders are willing to tolerate.

Leaders say that standards must be upheld, but the moment of truth is what happens when one of those standards is violated.

What action takes place, or does not take place, says everything to the rest of the organization.

By the way, if the person at the top of the organization is not living the prescribed culture through proper behaviors, there is no way that all other employees are either. Let that one sit for a moment. In a perfect world, the CEO will hold themself accountable. No one should be above the law when it comes to culture.

There are other signs of mediocrity in leadership:

Managers wait too long to address performance.

This is a classic tenet of a mediocre culture. Mediocre leaders wait to have critical conversations; when they do act, the approach is often too late. By that time, the message often comes across with a disciplinary tone.

Great leaders do not tolerate mediocre performance- they coach their employees to peak performance and step in and support them when they do not meet standards. Great leaders make tough choices when necessary- they will not keep an underperforming employee because they know it has impact on their high performers and the overall culture.

Another sign that trouble is afoot:

Managers avoid confrontation altogether.

Nothing screams mediocrity like avoidance. Mediocre

leaders avoid dealing with challenging situations because it is uncomfortable. Instead, they take the path of least resistance by accepting complacency and settling for less. Mediocre managers reward compliance rather than honesty and candidness. They do not speak up because they do not want to "rock the boat." Instead, they make excuses for low performers and are slow to act.

Influential leaders realize that although difficult conversations are uncomfortable, they are necessary for creating a high-performance culture. They focus on the bigger picture by dealing with issues early so they do not develop into more considerable challenges. Exceptional leaders are bold and courageous leaders.

I am sure you are reading this and thinking that this is all logical, this makes sense, and indeed every leader knows this. I agree, but it is all in the execution. It is about that decisive moment-what a leader does when the situation is right in front of them.

Here is another marker of mediocrity:

Managers like doing technical work, not leadership work.

There is a philosophy called "The Freedman Model." Developed by Professor Alan Freedman, it is described as the Transformation Trilogy- Add On, Preserve, and Let Go. Critical skill requirements change as your career progresses through different organizational levels. As you advance from technical roles to leadership roles to strategic positions, the demands change from short-term to longer-term, from managing tasks to managing a network of key stakeholders. The changing needs require a changing set of skills.

New skills must be added to their repertoire, existing strengths must be preserved, and vestigial skills must be let go. This Add On, Preserve, and Let Go approach is critical to assess when moving into a role with a higher level of responsibility. In fact, by the time you reach an executive-level position, your success is almost entirely driven by your ability to develop and implement strategy.

The "Let Go" part is often the toughest for leaders. Letting go means giving up the things you love to do. It is also about letting go of those things that comfort you and make you feel competent when the new role gets challenging. The bottom line is that more leadership is required when you ascend to a leadership role.

Mediocre leaders spend far too much time putting out fires, dealing with interruptions, and drowning themselves in lower-level technical work. They often complain that they lack time to coach employees, give feedback, plan, or be strategic. Most mediocre leaders do not enjoy the "leadership work" and would much rather deal with technical work because they equate their value with their specialized expertise. And this is precisely why they are not effective leaders.

Exceptional leaders spend more time thinking about the future, asking clarifying questions, coaching their employees through challenges, and communicating a clear path. They avoid the temptation to get drawn into the technical work they are an expert in.

Yet another mediocre leadership identifier:

Managers are traditional.

Mediocre managers employ a command-and-control style of leadership. They do not see the importance or value of employee engagement. Mediocre managers also do not see the value in feedback, empathy, coaching, or appreciation. Instead, they tend to micromanage and drive results through fear.

Years ago, I recalled a leader saying, "If I cannot get respect, I settle for fear." He was in a regional director position then, and fifteen years later, he is still a regional director. He never equated his lack of people development to his lack of development.

Influential leaders understand that employee engagement leads to higher productivity, which leads to results. Therefore, exceptional leaders spend time coaching, appreciating, supporting, and developing their employees.

Let me touch on one more point- a critical area:

With mediocrity, you will have a tough time keeping high performers.

Mediocre managers create mediocre teams. They accept complacency, so high performers become frustrated by the lack of progress and results. As I mentioned earlier in the chapter, high performers adjust their level of effort to meet the mediocrity of others around them or leave the organization. Since mediocre managers are average, they do not instill higher performance levels in their staff.

Exceptional leaders set clear standards and deadlines and expect their employees to work at a high level. They positively challenge their teams and reward them for hard work. They focus more on ensuring they keep their best employees and convey that average performance is unacceptable.

To support these principles, a high-performance culture must start with the actions of the top leaders in the organization.

It takes bold and courageous CEOs, executives, and managers to step up and change the temperature setting of the culture and declare that mediocrity is no longer acceptable. Exceptional leaders do not just talk about creating a high-performing culture; they take the actions necessary to make it.

Leadership is not easy. It requires a consistent focus on people and the greater organization. It requires having courageous conversations for the sake of the culture. Exceptional leaders are the caretakers, and they understand that every decision they make, or do not make, has a lasting impact on the culture.

Mediocre performance is a virus. Once an individual becomes infected, it spreads quickly to others; before long, it brings everyone down, crippling your team's chance of peak performance.

How you choose to manage the onset of mediocrity is of vital importance to the future health of your team. First, as the leader, you should ask yourself if you are part of the problem. Have you lowered your standards? Are you more tolerant of people not meeting your expectations than you used to be? Are you setting the right example? Has your passion or drive dropped?

Most mediocre performance is often a direct result of the leader's performance. I know that hurts. That is a hard leadership pill for most to swallow. But it tends to be true. You are likely to have played a part in the performance slump of your team.

Again, this is not a self-help book; it is a self-reflection book. Nothing will change if I do not give it to you straight.

I have been fascinated over the years watching executives wax poetically in public about the need for "accountability" and "high performance," then complain helplessly in private about one or two middling team members. You have no moral authority to ask other managers to hold people accountable if you are not doing so yourself.

Unfortunately, if you are hoping for a silver bullet to address mediocre performance, I have little to offer except for this statement and these subsequent four principles:

Chronic mediocrity is a symptom of ineffective leadership, not incapable personnel.

This sounds like gloom and doom, but mediocrity is not destiny. I have seen teams dramatically turn around their performance in a matter of months. They do it through four leadership practices that lead to performance excellence:

Show the consequences of mediocrity.

Your first job as a leader is to ensure everyone is crystal clear about what they are doing and why. Mediocrity is typically the result of a disconnection between someone's work and the consequences and impact of their performance.

Find ways to connect people with the impact of good and bad performance. For example, keep the human connection alive by telling stories illustrating work well done. Avoid impersonal and bureaucratic language when talking about performance; frame your work in human terms whenever possible.

Use concrete measures as an influence.

Mediocrity often hides behind undefined and unclear measures. In contrast, meaningful actions make mediocre performance painfully apparent. Every organization and every department within every organization should have key performance indicators. These KPIs should be common language amongst the organization and a clear and tangible way to measure performance.

Ideally, these metrics are "excuse resistant." Business changes will not impact the effectiveness of the correctly identified key performance indicators. When it is understood that there is a level playing field for performance, you will have the attention of everyone on the team. Most will be motivated to achieve those results, and those who are not will find excuses. You will know all you need to know at that point to address performance.

Establish peer accountability.

Mediocrity is also often a sign of solid supervision. That may sound counterintuitive, so stay with me here. I have found that a strong leader can mute the voice of weaker leaders and, in turn, mask their ineptitude.

On top-performing teams, peers immediately and respectfully confront one another when problems arise.

Once you have helped the team connect with what they do and why and established key performance metrics, peer accountability becomes an important next step. Regular reviews allow mutual feedback and establish peer accountability as a routine occurrence.

Speak up.

For high performance to become a cultural norm, it must be defended regularly and vigilantly.

There is an elephant in the room. As the leader, it is your job to address these situations, especially if no one else will. If a corporate initiative is an utter but undiscussable failure, your team will watch whether you have the integrity to point out that the emperor has no clothes. If you have a chronically poor performer on the team, everyone will also watch the handling of that situation. If you shrink from or delay addressing this issue, you send a message to everyone else about your values.

One final point here:

Mediocrity is the biggest threat to greatness, especially in a business setting. Mediocrity, though, for all its challenges, is relatively easy to spot and easy to measure.

Indifference, however, does not come wrapped neatly in measurable key performance indicators. Instead, indifference is much more abstract and, as a result, more dangerous in many ways.

CHAPTER 2:

The Trouble With Indifference

Because of the abstract nature of indifference, it is difficult to define it through principles, so I will explain indifference through storytelling.

But, before I get into the details, I need to disclaim this chapter- there are some graphic elements. To be clear, I am not disclaiming this chapter because I am apologetic. No, just the opposite- I have had opportunities to back away from the content, but I chose not to.

I want this chapter to get your attention; I need this chapter to get your attention.

I defined indifference earlier in the book, but that is a literary interpretation. I am okay with it, but here is what I think about when I contemplate indifference:

Indifference is the ethical and moral ability to look away, do nothing... and be okay with it.

Often, in our society, we turn to look at the things that we are curious about that, arguably, we should not be looking at, i.e., a car accident that occurs along our path. The phenomenon of mostly everyone stepping on the brakes to look at what is a tragic situation or worse- a potential death of other human beings- is concerning. It is troubling. No matter what your reason, or excuse, for slowing down to look, it does not pass the decency test.

Of course, it is easy to blame it on the car in front of you because that person stepped on their brakes first. However, a car at the front of it all slowed down to start the chain reaction, so at least one person fits the despicable profile that I am describing.

Nothing positive comes from stopping to look. Other than arriving on the scene first to help, the most respectful thing to do is to keep it moving. Often though, the rest of us step on our brakes. Surely, your seven seconds of staring at what happened are not what caused the traffic to back up. I assure you that the fifty cars before you said the same thing too. Of course, others will say that it was the police lights that caused them to brake. Oh, okay. Only you know your level of nosiness.

This balking behavior to look at an accident is troubling enough; even more disturbing is when we do the opposite and turn away from the things that should get our attention- like crime and injustice.

When we look away from those things, we become bystanders.

There are many reasons why we become a bystander, so I am not going to judge you and the decisions that you have made- that is up to you to assess after reading this chapter.

Again, the displaced curiosity that we have about other people's tragedy, but conversely demonstrating the lack of empathy to help relieve the pain of another person's tragedy, is a situation that troubles me. When this lack of empathy occurs, we stand indifferent.

For those who have invested time and expense to read my writings, I appreciate and recognize that many of you may share the same views as I do... and I do not mean political or religious beliefs. I am talking about something higher than that- morality and ethics. You know, with things like a general agreement that murder is wrong.

I want to take this conversation to a higher level of civility. I hope to reach you intellectually, but reaching you emotionally is far more critical.

I know most of us believe we are balanced and objective. Most of us think we are "independents" in politics and "we listen to all types of music." You might as well say that we are all "good drivers."

It is time to get real; I mean, really real. If you have a bias about something- if you are racist, homophobic, or do not like tall people, whatever it is, just own it. If we really were without biases, this 'I am balanced' posturing means we would have a homogenous, like-minded United States of America. We are clearly not that, but we should continue to strive for that. As is written, 'in order to form a more perfect union.'

So, allow me to break down indifference and then get into a few stories.

Indifference is a state in which we do not care enough to act on something happening around us. Perhaps, even worse, we wait for someone else to remedy the situation... and there are times when that other person never comes.

Let me give a business parallel to this, as it is essential to address indifference head-on, no matter if you are at home or work.

In the work environment, over the years, I have noticed employees who often say things about senior management like, "They don't get it" or "What were they thinking to introduce this new policy or product?" We know context matters; making changes and not telling people why is always a recipe for disaster. You also want people to see the reason for change so that their only negative response can be 'I don't agree,' not 'I didn't know.' More on the latter reaction in the next chapter.

For this discussion, sometimes "they" is not always a reference to the executive leadership team- it could be a district manager or regional vice president. However, do not be deceived- the executive team is never excluded from the description of "they."

My point here is that employees say this all the way through their development journey until, one day, they realize they are "they." My second point is that once you are "they," you can do something about situations- you now have positional power.

You may say, I get it, but what about when you do not have this positional power to affect things around you? You then rely on personal power- the ability to influence through relationships and persuasion.

The bottom line is this: what often holds us back may not be positional power, personal power, or even fear; it is indifference: the belief that I cannot impact a situation, or worse, no desire to.

To that end, if there was another rung to performance of the levels I referenced in the previous chapter, there would be a level below poor performance; it would be indifference. Yes, indifference is more complicated to measure, like great, good, mediocre, and poor performance, but also far more concerning... especially if you believe that poor behaviors lead to poor performance.

So, how do we get to this place of indifference?

One cause may be that we are overstimulated, which can quickly happen in today's culture. We receive information on our phones all day and all night- we are often on high alert for current information. We are bombarded with horrible news from around the world at the very moment it occurs.

Indifference may also occur when the problems in our life, families, communities, country, and world seem so overwhelming that we feel powerless to do anything about them. Instead of trying, we shrug our shoulders and move on. Even when a problem is directly within our path to address, we may pass on the actual or perceived responsibility to engage.

You may be unconcerned about the little things- like what to eat for dinner, what to watch on television, or whether you decide to go to the gym. However, when we become indifferent about the important things, it may be time for self-examination.

Indifference can and often shows up in one of the most critical aspects of our lives- relationships. In a relationship, when there are signs that things are headed downward, there will often be evidence of indifference. Things like arguing stops. That is a sure sign of problems ahead when one or both people in the relationship decide that even arguing is not worth it, that silence is a better option. It sounds like a resolution, but it is more of a resignation... and a signal of more trouble to come.

Indifference also appears in areas of our life that seem important to our livelihood, yet many people pass on taking action due to a lack of belief that their input will matter. Here is one of those areas:

Let's examine presidential voting in the United States- please put away your political flags for a moment. The perspective that I often hear people say is, "Why should I vote? It is not going to matter anyways." They are not wrong. I will not lecture about the Electoral College, although I probably should. In most states, this statement has been proven to be true. Unless you are a "swing state," as a citizen, your vote in the historical minority party in your state will be swallowed up and rendered meaningless. Perhaps the fact that we have the term "swing state" is a problem, but I will resist the urge to stray here too.

Take Kentucky, for example, my birth state. Kentucky has been Republican for as long as I can remember and predominately Republican for the past six Presidential elections. In that state, your Democratic vote literally does not count.

Okay, I cannot resist- we could overhaul the Electoral College. But I am not confident that will happen in my lifetime... or ever. I am not sure Wyoming, no disrespect, should get two senators like a state sixty-eight times more populous, like California. I have read the reason- so that smaller states get fair representation. Really? It seems like you would give every state one Senator, and even that is a stretch, and divide the other fifty Senator slots based on population. I apologize for being so practical. The apathy of voting stems from logic, or a lack of logic, like this.

By the way, the presidential election every four years in the United States is still not a national holiday, thus making it harder to get off work and vote, and you cannot vote by mail everywhere, and you cannot vote on your phone. We can do anything else on our phones but vote for a president. I can flood reality talent shows on television with votes in mere seconds, but, apparently, the math to tabulate a president is different and much more challenging to manage. And then there is the popular vote. If every vote counted, every vote would count. I am not the most intelligent person on this topic, but it would seem that whoever gets the most votes in total would be the election's winner... but that is not how that works either. I am glad my children are adults because I am unsure I could explain it to a ten-year-old. I do not get it- I am always willing to bet on logic. But, seriously, how did we get here?

This is the procedural stuff that causes indifference, which causes everyday people to shrug their shoulders and walk away.

And then there is the actual human cost of indifference.

The story I want to share gets to the heart of indifference and its intersection with the human experience.

This will also get at being a bystander.

First, though, there was a movie some twenty-five years ago called 'A Time To Kill' starring Samuel L. Jackson, Sandra Bullock, and an up-and-coming actor named Matthew McConaughey.

The movie 'A Time To Kill' is not directly based on a true story, but close enough... and that is why it is relevant to this conversation.

The real-life crime that inspired John Grisham to write 'A Time To Kill' had remained a secret since he began writing it decades ago.

"It was one of those crimes you never forget," said Grisham in a later interview, who began his career as a lawyer in a Memphis law firm. This crime was so heinous that Grisham prayed that he would not get appointed to represent the defendant. Imagine that- most young attorneys cannot wait to get the high-profile case that could catapult their career. Not this lawyer and not this case.

While attending the University of Mississippi law school, Grisham had dreamed of becoming a big-time trial lawyer, but the real world had proved far more daunting.

Grisham heard about the crime before he read it in the newspaper. News of this crime stunned him. "It was terrible," he said. "I never did want to represent a defendant in a rape case. And I sure did not want that one."

Instead, the judge appointed Grisham's classmate, and Grisham was spared the despicable job of overseeing this case. Brace yourself:

In an interview, Grisham recounted the case he watched involving the 1984 rapes of two white teenage sisters in a remote farmhouse only a few miles from his law office.

"One day, I stumbled upon a horrible trial in which a young girl testified against a man who brutally raped her. It was a gut-wrenching experience, and I was only a spectator. One moment she was courageous; the next, she was pitifully frail. I was mesmerized. I could not imagine the nightmare she and her family had been through. I wondered what I would do if she were my daughter. As I watched the jury, I wanted personally to shoot the rapist. For one brief yet interminable moment, I wanted to be her father. I wanted justice."

"I became obsessed with the idea of a father's retribution. What would a jury of ordinary people do to such a father? Naturally, there would be a great deal of sympathy, but would there be enough for an acquittal?"

Back to the actual case: Deputies arrested the perpetrator, a Black man named Willie James Harris, who confessed. Days later, Grisham heard the confession on tape, where Harris shared the details of the assault with all the emotion of reading items off a restaurant menu.

During a break, Grisham said he stared at Harris, thinking the defendant would be dead if he had been the father and had a gun.

The jury ultimately convicted Harris, who was sentenced to life without parole.

Grisham's anger led him to wonder- what would a jury do to a father who killed his daughter's rapist?

The case was so "gut-wrenching" for Grisham that he made a material change to the storyline. Race.

This was the birth of 'A Time To Kill.'

Driving back one day from the state Capitol in Jackson to his home in Southaven, Grisham decided to capture the story forming in his mind.

In 1996, fledgling actor Matthew McConaughey played the lead as the good-guy lawyer in the John Grisham adaptation, "A Time to Kill."

In this movie, Samuel L. Jackson plays the despondent father of a little Black girl who is raped. That was material to the movie as it was filmed in a deep South, racially charged environment where slavery was no longer legal, but the remnants of it lingered much longer than the national footprint of change. It was common in this place and time for lynchings of Black people to still occur, and where Black people charged with crimes were judged by a jury of twelve white people.

As Matthew McConaughey's character is making his closing argument for the defendant, played by Samuel L. Jackson, he makes a very graphic statement. Here is what he says to the jury:

"I want to tell you a story. I am going to ask you all to close your eyes while I tell you the story. I want you to listen to me. I want you to listen to yourselves. Go ahead. Close your eyes, please. This story is about a little girl walking home from the grocery store one sunny afternoon. I want you to picture this little girl. Suddenly a truck races up. Two men jump out and grab her. They drag her into a nearby field, tie her up, and they rip her clothes from her body. Now they climb on. First one, then the other, raping her, shattering everything innocent and pure with a vicious thrust in a fog of drunken breath and sweat. And when they are done, after they have killed her tiny womb, murdered any chance for her to have children, to have a life beyond her own, they decide to use her for target practice. They start throwing full beer cans at her. They throw them so hard that it tears the flesh all the way to her bones. Then they urinate on her. Now comes the hanging. They have a rope. They tie a noose. Imagine the noose going tight around her neck, and with a sudden blinding jerk, she is pulled into the air, and her feet and legs go kicking. They do not find the ground. The hanging branch is not strong enough. It snaps, and she falls back to the earth. So, they pick her up, throw her in the back of the truck and drive out to Foggy Creek Bridge, and pitch her over the edge. And she drops some thirty feet down to the creek bottom below. Can you see her? Her raped, beaten, broken body soaked in their urine, soaked in their semen, soaked in her blood, left to die. Can you see her? I want you to picture that little girl. Now, imagine she is white."

A gasp came over the courtroom as the jury opened their eyes. A moment of introspection. A moment about race, a moment about civility, but also a moment about indifference.

I believe Grisham changed the race of the characters to get people to challenge their own biases- my words, not his. I also think the intention was to get an emotional reaction from all involved or bore witness to the trial. A reaction that should only lead to one conclusion:

Allowing, dismissing, siding with, or any stance other than utter disgust, which leads to action, is the seed of indifference.

The movie inferred that the two white rapists would not be convicted of killing a Black girl in the Deep South with an all-white jury. That was believable at that time in that setting... and almost everyone was okay with that. Indifference.

Sometimes, our biases take over, the peer pressure from family or friends to "be a certain way," and other environmental factors keep us from openly condemning acts that fall well outside the "reasonable person standard."

I must step away from the story to talk about this "reasonable person standard"- it is material.

I often apply the "reasonable person standard" to assess situations around me and how people respond to those situations. This term is frequently used in tort and Criminal law to denote a hypothetical person in society who exercises average care, skill, and judgment in conduct and serves as a comparative standard for determining liability. It is boring to many people, but following this principle often keeps us out of moral turpitude.

Here is an example: an Academy Award-winning actor stepping on the stage to slap a comedic host for telling a joke about his wife during one of the biggest telecasts in the world, outside of maybe the Super Bowl, is unreasonable. Of course, that would never happen in real life, right?

Invoking the reasonable person standard provides a range of acceptable responses, including yelling profanities or, more professionally, handling off-stage during a commercial break. On the other hand, charging on stage and assaulting the host is unreasonable. The reasonable person standard does not consider justification. Allowing justification broadens the definition and range of the reasonable person standard and, in some regards, renders it meaningless.

In this instance, I recognize that the joke was directed at the actor's wife and deemed out-of-bounds. All I will say is that alopecia is not cancer. You cannot die from it, and plenty of wigs are available to manage its stigma. I get it, I am taking the hard line here, but we cannot allow justification to excuse uncivil acts. We just can't.

In this example, indifference showed up in a dramatic way as the actor, only a few minutes later, received an Academy Award. He did what? That is correct; no one dared to step up and say: not on my watch, not today. Your immediate actions force us to rescind the award. Nope, business as usual. Indifference.

Okay, back to the story.

The twist in the fictional story of 'A Time To Kill' is even more thought-provoking due to race and the dilemma of the father whose heart ached for losing his little girl. However, the father's emotions would not allow him to be a bystander. Compelling storyline.

Ultimately, should a father be acquitted of his actions in this situation? A reasonable person would understand the father's plight. However, it is not suitable to break the law under any circumstances. Compelling. You will have to watch the movie to get Grisham's take on it.

Now I will get to the main story of this chapter. It is a story about indifference. A story about George Stinney: there is a pretty good chance that you have never heard of him. Before authoring this book, I had not either.

Unfortunately, this is a true story.

In 1944, George Junius Stinney Jr., a young Black boy, lived in Alcolu, South Carolina, with his father, George Stinney Sr., mother Aimé, brothers John, 17, and Charles, 12, and sisters Katherine, 10, and Aimé, 7. Stinney's father worked at the town's sawmill, and the family resided in company housing. Alcolu was a small, working-class mill town where railroad tracks separated White and Black neighborhoods. The town was typical of small Southern towns of the time. Because schools and churches for White and Black residents were segregated, there was limited interaction between the races.

Again, this story is true... and this did happen in the United States... when George Stinney Jr. was 14 years old. Remember, he was 14 years old.

On March 23, 1944, the bodies of two young White girls, Betty June Binnicker and Mary Emma Thames, were discovered in a ditch in Alcolu, South Carolina. The girls had gone missing the day before, as they had never returned home the previous night. The bodies were discovered on the Black side of Alcolu. Binnicker and Thames suffered severe blunt force trauma, resulting in the penetration of both girl's skulls.

The girls were last seen riding their bicycles, looking for flowers. As they passed the Stinneys' property, they had asked George Stinney Jr. and his sister, Aimé, if they knew where to find "maypops," a local name for passionflowers. Aimé said she was with Stinney when the police later established that the murders occurred.

According to an article reported by the wire services on March 24, 1944, and published widely, the sheriff announced the arrest of "George Junius" and stated that the boy had confessed and led officers to 'a hidden piece of iron.'

George Stinney Jr. and his older brother John were arrested for murdering the girls. The police released John, age 17, but George was held in custody. According to a handwritten statement, Stinney's arresting officer was H.S. Newman, a Clarendon County deputy, who stated, "I arrested a boy by the name of George Stinney. He then confessed and told me where to find a piece of iron, about fifteen inches, where he said he put it in a ditch about six feet from the bicycle." No confession statement signed by Stinney is known to exist. The 14-year-old later claimed that the arresting officers starved him and bribed him with food to confess.

Following Stinney's arrest, his father was fired from his job at the local sawmill, and the Stinney family had to vacate their company housing immediately. The family feared for their safety. Stinney was detained at a jail in Columbia, fifty miles from Alcolu, due to the threat of lynching.

Stinney was questioned alone, without his parents or an

attorney. Although the Sixth Amendment guarantees legal counsel, this was not routinely observed until the United States Supreme Court's 1963 ruling in Gideon v. Wainwright explicitly required representation during criminal proceedings. This was 1944.

The entire proceeding against Stinney, including jury selection, took one day.

I am going to let that sit for a moment.

No matter what speed you read, I implore you to read this part of the chapter just a bit slower.

Stinney's court-appointed counsel was Charles Plowden, a tax commissioner campaigning for election to local office. Plowden did not challenge the three police officers who testified that Stinney confessed to the two murders. He also did not challenge the prosecution's presentation of two different versions of Stinney's verbal confession. In one version, the girls attacked Stinney after he tried to help one girl who had fallen in the ditch and killed them in self-defense. In the other version, he had followed the girls, first attacking Mary Emma and then Betty June. There is no written record of Stinney's confession apart from Deputy Newman's statement that Stinney provided a verbal confession.

Other than the testimony of the three police officers, prosecutors called three witnesses at trial: Reverend Francis Batson, who discovered the bodies of the two girls, and the two doctors who performed the post-mortem examination. In addition, the court allowed discussion of the "possibility" of rape due to bruising on Binnicker's genitalia. Stinney's counsel did not call any witnesses, did not cross-examine witnesses, and offered little or no defense. The trial presentation lasted two and a half hours.

Okay, I am going to let that sit for a moment too.

These are trial proceedings in the 1940s in, no disrespect meant, the unsophisticated South that could not be conducted at this level of warp speed today, with all the advanced tools that exist, like DNA testing.

Additionally, more than 1,000 Whites crowded the courtroom, but no Black people were allowed, not one. This is an important distinction as this concludes the parents of the 14-year-old boy were not even allowed in the courtroom.

As was typical then, Stinney was tried before an all-white jury. In 1944, most Black people in the South were prohibited from voting and, therefore, ineligible to serve on juries.

After deliberating for fewer than ten minutes, the jury found Stinney guilty of murder.

You know what I am going to say here- I will let this sit for a moment.

With the quick judgment by the jury, Judge Philip H. Stoll followed by sentencing Stinney to death by electrocution.

There is no trial transcript, and Stinney's counsel filed no appeal.

Between the time of Stinney's arrest and his scheduled execution, his parents were allowed to see him once after the trial, when he was held in the Columbia penitentiary. After that, they were not allowed to see him at any other time.

Stinney's family, churches, and the NAACP appealed to Governor Olin D. Johnston for clemency, given the boy's age. Governor Johnston refused to intervene... even though this was a 14-year-old boy.

Stinney was executed on June 16, 1944, at 7:30 p.m. A total of 84 days from when the crime was committed.

Yes, I must let this sit for a moment too.

Stinney was prepared for execution by electric chair, using a Bible, the irony of ironies, as a booster seat because Stinney was too small for the chair. Stinney stood five-foot one inch and just over ninety pounds at his death. His arms and legs were restrained with straps, securing his body to the chair. His father was only allowed to approach the electric chair to say his final words to his son, and an officer asked George if he had any last words to say before the execution took place, but he only shook his head. The executioner pulled a strap from the chair and placed it over George's mouth, causing him to break into tears, and he then put the face mask over his face, which did not fit him, as he continued sobbing. Witnesses reported that the oversized mask slid off the boy's face during the horrific moments, exposing his wide-eyed, tear-stricken face to the crowd.

And that was that. I do not mean to be so matter of fact. I am making a point here that the process was so matter of fact.

The only evidence, or a lack thereof, against the young boy was from the three police officers who testified that he admitted to the killings. No physical or DNA evidence pointed to Stinney, who received a guilty verdict after the speedy end-to-end, two-hour trial... with no witnesses.

When Stinney was executed by electric chair in June 1944, he became the youngest confirmed American to be sentenced to death and executed in the twentieth century.

Ultimately, I reference the races of all involved, but I am not sure that this case is as much about race as it is about indifference. I mean, sure, race was involved, but with a different sensitivity now from then Jim Crow-era South Carolina. The real issue is indifference- the ethical and moral ability to look away, do nothing... and be okay with it.

These are the times when it would be easier to be a fiction writer. I did not want to write about this real story but felt compelled. Indifference comes in many forms. As I mentioned earlier in the book, talking about insignificant things, like throwing away a piece of paper that you missed the can with, does not get the attention needed for this topic. I am not sure that a 14-year-old being electrocuted does it for everyone either, but I sure hope that it does.

The indifference of hundreds of people surrounding this case is sickening. How can you not stop this act? How can you not take action against this tidal wave of hatred? Someone had the moral responsibility and, by the way, the positional power to say no, not today, not on my watch. A judge, a governor, a police officer, an attorney, a reporter. Anyone courageous enough to ask, "What are we doing here?" How many people in that courtroom lamented the decision but did not speak up due to peer pressure, societal pressure, or any other cultural norm that likely suppressed their voice?

I am sure someone is reading this and thinking that was then and this is now. This type of thing could not happen in present times. And that is the mentality that allows indifference to walk straight in the front door. That Pollyanna attitude, or naivety, literally creates opportunistic moments for indifference. It is just easier to believe these things cannot happen. It is easier on our souls.

Back to the case. A motion was filed for a new trial on October 25, 2013... almost 70 years later.

In interviews surrounding the trial, there was a person named as the culprit, who is now deceased. And it was said by the family that there was a deathbed confession. The rumored perpetrator came from a well-known, prominent White family. A member, or members of that family, had served on the initial coroner's inquest jury, which had recommended that Stinney be prosecuted.

There is compelling evidence that George Stinney was innocent of the crimes for which he was executed in 1944. Yet, the prosecutor relied, almost exclusively, on one piece of evidence to obtain a conviction in this capital case: the unrecorded unsigned 'confession' of a 14-year-old who was deprived of counsel and parental guidance and whose defense lawyer shockingly failed to call any witnesses or to preserve his right of appeal.

Rather than approving a new trial, on December 16, 2014, circuit court Judge Carmen Mullen vacated Stinney's conviction. She ruled that he had not received a fair trial, as he was not effectively defended, and his Sixth Amendment rights had been violated. In addition, Mullen ruled that his confession was likely coerced and thus inadmissible. She also found that the execution of a 14-year-old constituted 'cruel and unusual punishment' and that his attorney 'failed to call exculpating witnesses or to preserve his right of appeal.' Finally, regarding the legal process, Mullen wrote, "No one can justify a 14-year-old child charged, tried, convicted, and executed in some 80 days," concluding, "In essence, not much was done for this child when his life lay in the balance."

A moment here to exhale. Maybe this could not happen in current-day America, but if you have a 14-year-old son, give him an extra big hug tonight.

I feel sick writing this chapter. I cry every time I re-read it. It leaves me to wonder whether I am just hypersensitive, and whether my reaction is representative of most people. I hope that my sentiment is similar to many others. I would rather feel something than not.

I believe we are better than this, better than everything I have written about in this chapter... and then there are times when we are not.

This story speaks to that pit in the back of your stomach. That achy feeling when you know something is not right, yet you do nothing to stop it. That is indifference. Whether intentional or not, that is indifference.

Indifference is not just a lack of emotion; indifference can also be a lack of action.

In the case of George Stinney Jr., the present-day version is acquiescing to eleven other jurors when you are called for jury duty when you know what the right thing is to do. A hung jury is better than allowing justice to be fractured.

In the end, eliminating indifference is vital to civility in our society. We must be compelled to act. Something that shows that we care- that other lives have meaning, that we feel something, like crying when we see other people's pain.

Just as I referenced with mediocrity earlier in the book, I do not believe anyone sets out to be indifferent. And the good news is that there are things that you can do about indifference.

Many will ask, "How can I be held accountable for something I did not do or do not know about?" Well, this story is not about accountability, and I am not expecting anyone to have ever heard this story. Again, I had not heard the story until recently.

However, the great thing about knowing is no longer not knowing. Therein lies what can be a confusing part of indifference- you are not held accountable for the past, but once you know, you should be held responsible for the future. So, you should be kicking and screaming for the right thing to be done- no matter where, no matter when, and no matter who.

Perhaps, the first step to eliminating indifference is once you do know about something is to stop saying, "I Didn't Know."

CHAPTER 3

I Didn't Know

You may have heard this quote before: "In the age of information, ignorance is a choice."

I will also say that in the age of information, knowledge is a choice.

What you know influences you. What you do not know sometimes has even more of an influence. However, what you do not know and choose not to hear or see are different. Ignorance is not always a lack of knowledge. Ignorance can be driven by the unwillingness to learn more.

While ignorance is a problem, I reference it only to make this point. There is a more significant problem to address... "I Didn't Know."

The connection here in this chapter is that these three words can lead to indifference and mediocrity... in a very damaging and lasting way. Also, the barriers created by "I Didn't Know" slam the brakes on learning new things.

There is a theme that I hope you are noticing in this book: The Depths Of Mediocrity is much more about behaviors than it is results; results are almost always a direct correlation to the behaviors exhibited. To that end, "I Didn't Know" is a behavior that is so cleverly disguised that you may not detect the insidious intentions.

"I Didn't Know" is the ultimate escape from responsibility. "I Didn't Know" creates the opportunity not to choose good or evil, love or hate, left or right, or deal with any other potentially polarizing moral or ethical topic. You can simply bail out of the pressure of taking a position by saying, "I Didn't Know."

"I Didn't Know" can be a bit disingenuous partly because it draws a direct line to indifference- a lack of care and, in this context, a lack of wanting to know the truth. It also creates a lack of awareness of the world around you- not impossible, but certainly harder to do in today's environment. I mean, virtually everyone has heard of the Kardashians, although I have heard people say that they have never heard of them. It does not mean you like them or like anything about them or have ever watched the show, but to say "I Didn't Know" when asked who they are just feels like an unnecessary lie.

One other point to put on this:

Saying "I Didn't Know" is as egregious as saying I did not hear something that was said in a room directly to you by the only other person in the room. Last time I checked, unless you are hard of hearing, you cannot "unhear" something. You can pretend, though.

Here is yet another challenge to overcome. This notion of "I Didn't Know" has been spurred on by terms like "Fake News." That should not be a political term, but I am sure some will interpret it as that. I promise you that when you read my books, there is no dog whistle or "read between the lines" stuff- I will tell you what I mean or think.

If you are holding a black pen that tells you on the packaging that it has black ink, and then you open the package and write with it, and it is a black line on the piece of paper, then it is black. That is a fact, and it is not fake or disputable.

The great news is that most people are reasonable and do not waste their time challenging facts, like whether a black pen is black. But, again, "I Didn't Know" is a bit of a loophole. It allows you to challenge others in a passive-aggressive way without really stating your position.

You know, like telling someone that former president Barack Obama graduated from Harvard and was elected the first black president of the Harvard Law Review or that former president George H. W. Bush became the only U.S. president to have previously held the position of Director of Central Intelligence as head of the CIA, which gave him a unique perspective on both giving and receiving intelligence. Do you see what I did there?

I covered both Democratic and Republican examples so that no one could paint me in a corner. Responding with "I Didn't Know" to either one of those massive accomplishments has potential shade written all over it, particularly if you do not like one or the other of the former presidents simply because of their political party. Perhaps, a proper response would be something like, "That is amazing!" Extraordinary accomplishments by both men.

Now, I will argue against myself. "I Didn't Know," in this instance, could be a very harmless statement. And I could be reading way too much into the potential nefarious intentions of the reaction to the information about the former presidents...

... and this is how it happens. We miss the subliminal messages; we automatically give people the benefit of the doubt. All I am recommending is to listen a bit more intently. "I Didn't Know" may not be what you think it is.

It could be that the person honestly didn't know, but this consistent response on topic after topic leads you back to the initial conversation in this chapter- ignorance. Again, not as intentional as "I Didn't Know," but still a problem.

I will digress for a moment. Referencing both former presidents reminded me of a moment involving both of them... together. My wife and I attended an event years ago in College Station, Texas, celebrating the Points of Life Institute that the first President Bush started when he was in office in 1992. This was the twenty-year celebration. Both former President Bush and the current president at that time, Barack Obama, were there together, and both spoke- a real-life celebration of the two parties coming together.

I had the pleasure of going backstage and meeting former President Bush before the event. It was one of those moments when you knew that you were in the presence of greatness. He was a very reserved and peaceful man and the leader he appeared to be from a distance. I always viewed him as a humanitarian more than as a president. That is why I voted for him the first time I was old enough to vote in 1988. I did not understand political parties at the time, and, in reflection, I am glad that I did not.

By the way, there was no chance of meeting President Obama as a sitting president at this event. Let's just say his security detail was a bit tighter.

It was an incredibly inspiring event. My wife and I could not wait to get home and turn on the television to see the event's coverage, and then... nothing- not even a mention of the event. It was as though it had never happened. If we had not been there, I am not sure that we would have believed anyone else if they had told us they had attended such an amazing event. The only conclusion we could draw to justify the absence of coverage of the event is that it was not sensational, divisive politics. Decency just does not sell the same.

Back to "I Didn't Know."

To rid ourselves of mediocrity and indifference, we must come face-to-face with our realities. I would never suggest what people should believe in, but our courts, colleges, and military are littered with words like honor, decorum, respect, courage, trust, etc. I suppose, on some level, we want these things in our democracy. Each word can be defined differently by person; therein lies the difficulty in getting to what I am describing with "I Didn't Know." It mainly falls apart when we cannot agree on simple things like the sun rises in the east and sets in the west every single day or attacking our U.S. Capitol is not a good thing.

Again, petty things like that.

This is where we have arrived in the present day. We are a highly combative society that is now taking sides in the most trivial of things, refusing to move from that position, and now threatening each other for not having that same position. I do not mean figuratively- people are actually willing to kill each other for their views. It is a troubling conversation and combination. Some historians say this is not unique, as conflict has always occurred. But, unfortunately, the present time for anything is usually adopted as the best or worst of times- that is just human nature.

That said, it does feel like there is just something different in the air right now- something different about post-pandemic times, something different about politics, something different about race relations, something different about gun control and gun violence, and most certainly something different about civility.

Of course, decades like the 1960s were no walks in the park, so my intent is not to minimize the seismic changes that occurred then, largely shaping the country that we are today.

Another example of "I Didn't Know' played out when I was at home one Sunday morning in 2016 with the television playing in the background. I was in and out of the room, cleaning and preparing for the week ahead. The show had a guest lamenting racial inequality in America. The guest was Bryan Stevenson.

If you do not know who Bryan Stevenson is, he founded the Equal Justice Initiative in Alabama and is the real-life motivation behind the true story of the powerful and thought-provoking movie "Just Mercy."

"Just Mercy" follows young lawyer Bryan Stevenson, played by Michael B. Jordan, and his history-making battle for justice. This excerpt from IMDb describes the plot: "After graduating from Harvard, Bryan could have had any job he wanted, but instead, he heads to Alabama to defend those wrongly condemned, with the support of local advocate Eva Ansley. One of his first and most incendiary cases is that of Walter McMillian, who, in 1987, was sentenced to die for the notorious murder of an 18-year-old girl, despite a preponderance of evidence proving his innocence and the fact that the only testimony against him came from a criminal with a motive to lie. In the following years, Bryan becomes embroiled in a labyrinth of legal and political maneuverings and overt and unabashed racism as he fights for Walter and others like him, with the odds and the system stacked against them."

That is Bryan Stevenson.

On the day I was listening to television, Bryan Stevenson evoked the word "genocide" in his remarks about race here in the United States.

Well, that was certainly different- I needed to hear more. Contextually, I had never heard the word genocide used in any conversation about race in America. Stevenson went on to contrast the difference between the Holocaust, the genocide in Rwanda in 1994, and the current state of race in America. It was an interesting take. His point was this:

If you visit present-day Germany, there are clear and present signs of the attempts by the German government to make amends for the past. When you go to Rwanda, there is unmistakable evidence of the government providing reparations to the many widowed women who were left to raise their families as their husbands were slaughtered in the genocide. However, in the United States, it is difficult to get anyone to acknowledge slavery, understand the implications of terms like lynching, move away from racial profiling, and other behaviors that have led to the current state of race.

Whether Stevenson is right or wrong, his take and involvement in race relations in the U.S. keep the topic at the forefront and remind us how far we still could go, with the right balance.

However, there is a cautionary tale here. No one should be held accountable for their ancestors or things that they did not personally do. In current times, White people in America have taken on that burden, including some friends of mine, and I believe that is categorically wrong. Black people, at times, have placed that responsibility on White people of today, which is even more unacceptable. Talking about the past does not have to come with guilt. In fact, it can have the opposite effect. The more we know, the more we can reconcile the past... and our views.

Here is another example of "I Didn't Know." I was flying back from Phoenix, Arizona, a few years ago, 2017, to be exact. I was flying with headphones in tow- the universal airplane sign that I did not want to talk to anyone. I ditched earbuds years earlier, as many people were not getting the hint. Any hard-working professional knows there is no better work time than being in the air- no one can reach you, but you can hammer out emails and get caught up.

A woman riding next to me did everything possible to engage in conversation, no matter how disinterested I appeared to be. I must admit, she was persistent. Persistent to the point that I finally had to take the headphones off and engage.

She made it clear that she wanted to discuss the Affordable Care Act. Of course, that led to politics.

After sharing her disdain for the Affordable Care Act, I felt inclined to respond. There is a lot I did not like about the Affordable Care Act either, but I happened to have a 22-year-old son at that time that I could cover on my insurance plan all the way through college. Opponents of the bill, including this woman, could not even admit that the addition of allowing coverage of dependent children through the age of 26 was a positive element of the ACA. I mean, what is the downside of that? Who wants to have a college senior at 22 years old working hard to finish their degree, but who, at the same time, must go out and find healthcare coverage? Well, it has never made sense, but that is what we have been doing for generations. But this is where she was- arguing for the sake of arguing. And following a prevailing government sentiment at that time, if you cannot fix a problem perfectly, do not try to fix it at all.

Of course, her response to learning that the ACA expanded child coverage to age 26 was, "I Didn't Know."

It was frustrating, but in our daily walk, we will encounter those who are equipped with incorrect information and, at the same time, are often the loudest voice in the room.

As I stated earlier, indifference is more than not caring. Indifference is also about not caring about knowing.

Ultimately, this was "I Didn't Know" on an exceedingly small scale. I will shift gears here because this chapter is not all about politics and race. It is also about perspective, but perspective is often cloaked in social issues. The perspective that was to come next related to "I Didn't Know" was more profound.

"I Didn't Know" was also underpinned in the conversation about Colin Kaepernick and why he was kneeling during the national anthem. By the way, his decision to kneel had nothing to do with patriotism, the national anthem, or disrespect for the military. In fact, Kaepernick was advised by a former military member that this approach of kneeling during the national anthem was the way to go and in no way disrespectful. Admittedly though, Kaepernick is at least partly to blame for hitching his message to the ceremony celebrating the American flag- that was an unwise decision, no matter the counsel given. So, I do not believe Kaepernick could run from the responsibility for the link people made.

However, I am purposely playing the middle here. It still does not change Kaepernick's intention, which the "other side" should at least acknowledge. His actions were meant to be an expression about police brutality and racial injustice, zeroing in on a country allowing unarmed Black motorists to be repeatedly killed by armed, White officers for something as simple as a broken taillight. That is it, and that is all.

Kaepernick's message got hijacked, and the conflation began to connect his message to this manufactured patriotism message, and the rest is history. Oh well, hopefully, you knew that already.

One bias influencing how people feel about this subject is the unwavering support for the military in our country. I am emphasizing unwavering here as the military often has support, no matter the behavior that is demonstrated. Based on what our armed forces do to protect us, disrespecting them in any way should not be accepted. The national anthem is just too close of a link between real patriotism and our military to be compromised.

On another note, this unwavering support also exists for police. I am not sure that should be the case... based on police behaviors.

Having a conversation about police, in general, in this country is difficult. Everyone knows that the majority of people serving as police officers are living up to their oath to protect and serve. I believe that almost all of them want their communities to be safe, and they take their responsibility very seriously.

The breakdown often comes when none of the police can be criticized. There are bad police officers, plain and simple. The evidence, at times, is overwhelming. Whether 1% or 20% of police officers are corrupt is an honest debate that we should be able to have.

This next point may or may not be a proxy for this conversation about police corruption.

Police brutality goes well beyond traffic stops. Unfortunately, it is often extended to the bedroom.

There is this headline: Law Enforcement officers beat their significant others at nearly double the national average. Several studies indicate that women suffer domestic abuse in at least forty percent of police officer families. For American women overall, the figure is closer to twenty-five percent, according to the Centers for Disease Control and Prevention.

Another data point: According to The Advocates for Human Rights Organization, studies indicate that police families are two to four times more likely than the general population to experience domestic violence, making the potential for disparities in protective success particularly troubling.

I get it; beating your wife or girlfriend is different from Kaepernick's assertion of killing defenseless and unarmed Black men, but it does make a link to the same person being violent.

I know some will debate the facts and miss the point here, so let me state it again: Women married to male police officers, the overwhelming majority of all cases of police brutality, are assaulted twice as much as other women, by those who are allegedly supposed to protect them the most.

I am not asking you to do anything with this information, except to say, now you know. You just literally read this, so the next time you are in a conversation, this topic comes up, and someone shares similar data, I would hope that you would not respond with, "I Didn't Know."

This is not about making a point here. I am simply emphasizing that the phrase "I Didn't Know" can create an unnecessary and biased barrier preventing the actual conversation. Backing away from this three-word statement is backing away from its bias. That is a powerful change to enact in our daily walk.

I recognize that my own biases come out in my writings, and I find evidence to prove it- that is what we do as humans, but I am working to get as close to objectivity as possible.

In the end, the only way to genuinely appreciate "I Didn't

Know" is to stay on the path of curiosity. Life can challenge your preconceived notions of the world around you.

Again, this is not just about a lack of knowledge- we cannot possibly know everything on our life journey. However, once you do know, you cannot unknow it.

There is a greater force than knowledge; it is called wisdom. Wisdom is knowledge applied.

While you could say that ignorance has always been a matter of choice, it is even more true with the incredible advancements in technology that have been made. Meaning that, now, more than ever, ignorance is not something we should be so quick to accommodate or accept. Accessing the truth is closer than ever before in our lives. We should seek it out.

Finally, do not allow people to get away with phrases like, "I Didn't Know." Also, do not let people throttle your disdain for indifference by injecting statements like "It could have been worse," "I have seen worse," or "you should have seen it before I got here" as a way to minimize the damage of something that has gone horribly wrong. These direct or indirect comparisons lend themselves to more mediocrity and more indifference.

In fact, comparisons come with their own risks.

CHAPTER 4:

Comparatively Speaking

I discussed greatness in an earlier chapter. Greatness stands on its own- it does not need to be compared to anything else. Greatness does not look back to see who is chasing it- greatness continues to focus on greatness. Comparing any situation to another can lower the bar so far that you open the door to indifference and mediocrity.

This chapter is designed to expose comparisons for what they are and explore their danger.

The definition of comparison is about similarities and differences between two or more things. That is the literal definition.

In practice, we often use comparisons to say that one thing is better than another thing.

Growing up, we begin making comparisons as soon as we learn what it means to want something or to keep out of trouble.

That is acceptable when you are five years old and complaining that your big brother got one more cookie than you did. But, of course, at five years old, the rationing of cookies is pretty darn important. However, we cannot act like a petulant five-year-old as adults and leaders.

For example, we are expected to be more responsible and not say to a police officer when we are pulled over for speeding, "Well, the car next to me was speeding too." Not a good moment to make a comparison.

Of course, we also see it in other areas of life, like sports. A basketball coach complaining about a foul call and comparing it to a call that was not made by the referee earlier in the game. How many of those calls are overturned due to the coach throwing a five-year-old-type tantrum? Well, the answer is none of them.

So, be careful. It is tempting to compare, but comparisons can sound five-year-oldish, never get overturned, and the warning that the police officer was going to give you gets turned into a full-fledged ticket or, worse, an escorted ride to the local lockup.

Comparing yourself or your situation to someone else's situation means that this is your best, which could be a low bar, and you are a nose ahead of the next person. This can land you in the murkiness of mediocrity.

There is a subconversation to have about comparisons. Coming to this point now- one of them is the notion of "the weakest link." No, I am not referring to the television show from years ago with the same name, if you are old enough to remember that from the early 2000s.

I am talking about the person making the least contribution to the collective achievement of a group. This is different from a weak link. To the point of the term weak link, many will argue that everyone on the team is performing... including the person at the bottom of the list. The term the weakest link does not allow for that. The weakest link is a force rank, plain and simple-someone is on the bottom. So, the clarity of the term weakest link versus weak link is material.

By the way, this applies not only to a work setting; this could also be an issue in your family unit. Uh oh, I think I have your attention now, but I promise I am not trying to create any family drama. I will come back to this.

What I have found most fascinating is that, in almost every situation, everyone on a team can identify the weakest link. I say almost always because often the person who does not know who the weakest link is is the person who is the weakest link. Even more tantalizing, the team is waiting for the leader to do something about it. But, again, this could be the head of a household, not only the leader of a workgroup.

The weakest link on your team, in your office, in your circle of friends, or even amongst your family is not always publicly called out, like being the last person chosen in a pick-up basketball game, but trust me, everyone knows who the weakest link is. And not that I have ever been the last one selected in a pick-up basketball game. Well, maybe...

I am going to be intentionally redundant here. The weakest link is not some conjectural philosophy. By sheer nature of force rank, there is always a "weakest link." I do not want this to be wordplay, so I am using this word specifically. A "weak link" and the "weakest link" are different. A weak link allows for another type of comparison and relieves you of the responsibility of force ranking. The weakest link requires you to put things, in this case, people, in order. Ultimately, there is a bottom.

I know that force ranking anything does not feel good. Still, it does allow you to begin to break apart and analyze situations to minimize the chances of mediocrity and indifference.

Comparisons give you an out- a reason not to address the weakest link. Unless you go all the way to force rank and determine if one person or one thing does not belong and you could identify that it would be the first person or thing removed, you have not gone far enough. I know it sounds harsh, but again, comparisons make you feel good, but they do not get to the heart of the issue.

Okay, back to the family drama reference earlier. We are often more emotionally invested in our families than in friends and work connections- a general statement that can be challenged. I get it but go with my example here.

Emotions can change everything. Regarding family, the feeling of choosing which child to let go of comes to mind. However, the weakest link is not that difficult of a decision, and here is why:

Comparisons are often clouded with emotion, and relationship strength can skew your judgment. There is always a human element. That said, I bet you could choose which of your children is the weakest link if you had to. I am not saying that you would like it.

All that said, of course, even work relationships can be complex; we become invested in people we work with for many reasons, not the least of which is a function of how much time we may spend at work.

I have my own experience of a work-related comparison. Early in my career, I hired a gentleman named Benjamin. To put it plainly, Benjamin was the best human being I ever hired, but the worst hiring decision I ever made. I know, I need to explain this statement.

I managed a retail store, and Benjamin was hired as an Assistant Manager. In reflection, Benjamin was a bit light on managerial experience but remarkably high on ambition. I needed to build a new team for the long term, so it made sense that some of the group could take longer than others to develop based on various experience levels. Benjamin was clearly the weakest link on the team. Unfortunately, it did not take long to find this out.

Benjamin was progressing slowly through the management-in-training work, which was relatively basic- counting down register tills, making deposits, operating the point-of-sale register, etc. We had not begun the tasks of writing schedules, conducting inventories, writing reviews, or reviewing financials. We were at the ground level of management work and Benjamin was struggling mightily.

It became clear that the gap was a cognitive issue- Benjamin was mentally unable to process the tasks required to perform the most basic functions of the role of an Assistant Manager. It indeed was a grey matter issue... and, in some ways, it made the situation even more challenging to manage.

I felt bad. I felt responsible. And you know what? I should have.

First, the management team I had at the time was fragile and needed an overall upgrade. I had only been in that store in that role for three months, so I was attempting to change everything at once. Second, I convinced myself I had not hired Benjamin just to fill a spot and that his skill level was not so far from the rest of the management team. That may be true, but, in the end, it does not matter, as Benjamin would have been unable to perform the job on a fully functional, higher-performing team. In fact, it would have only highlighted his deficiency even more.

I spent most of every day that Benjamin worked correcting his mistakes or painstakingly walking him through the same procedures I had just trained him on the day before.

Another point of reflection- I was determined to prove my decision was right, so making Benjamin successful had an ulterior motive. However, it was still not the driver of my determination, as I generally felt terrible for Benjamin and wanted to see him have a personal breakthrough.

The relevant point here, as it relates to comparisons, is that my fatal flaw at the time was comparing Benjamin to the rest of the weak leaders on the team. Again, Benjamin was in the range of performance of the rest of the group, so I allowed myself at the time to say, "he is not so bad." If I had indeed gone through a force rank exercise, I would have been more inclined to address his performance sooner versus later. But, unfortunately, Benjamin was not in that job very long. Whatever the amount of time that Benjamin worked there, it was likely shorter than I remembered- simply because every day was a long day.

I am not sure what happened to Benjamin after he left. But, unfortunately, I felt like he would have an ongoing struggle in life, and perhaps he would not come across enough patient people to help see him through. Maybe though, he found just what he was looking for.

Overall, one of the principles that leaders struggle with is the notion of force rank. We do not use the term force rank in our everyday personal life, and yet, that is precisely what we are doing with decisions that we make with the limited time we have to make them.

Ultimately, the weakest link leads to continuous improvement.

If you buy into the philosophy of it, there is always someone or something that can be improved at the bottom, creating a new weakest link, and the process starts all over again.

So, you may be saying, what does any of this have to do with mediocrity? As I concluded the last chapter, mediocrity begins when you start saying things like, "I am not as bad as the person before me" or "You should have seen it when I got here." These are comparative statements... and markers of mediocrity.

There is still much more to discuss. But first, let's explore some of the outcomes of comparisons.

I remember the first time I compared myself to someone- I was in first grade. Of course, before attending school, it never dawned on me to compare myself to my siblings. School raised the stakes. The peer pressure, the judgment, the desire to impress... oh yes, the joys of school.

Middle school was the most relevant time of comparison for me, even more than the dreaded judgment of high school.

I was in middle school when I played sports for the first time. Payless Shoe Source was one of the most popular shoe stores in the U.S. at the time. Wait, actually, it was not. Payless happened to be the only shoe store that we could afford. As a family, we did not have much money, so I thought Payless was the best shoe store.

Playing basketball was all about the look and especially the shoes. This was pre-Michael Jordan Nike, but even back then, everyone already knew the swoosh... and everyone knew that my shoes were upside down. Yes, that is what I said. The Payless athletic shoe logo was an upside-down Nike swoosh. That is wrong on every level.

If anyone believed in my game, that perspective went out the window when they saw my shoes; in retrospect, I would have been so much happier with good-old Chuck Taylor's, Converse, that is.

I played basketball every day. I looked the part. I dribbled well, but my shoes were a considerable disadvantage. I often was called for traveling- walking with the ball without dribbling- during games. I was not actually traveling. My Payless shoes had no grip, so I slid everywhere. I thought the referee would pity me and look the other way as I glided through the lane.

It is often said that school does not prepare you for adulthood. There is some truth to that, I suppose. I mean, we do not learn about credit, credit scores, how to write checks, how to do laundry, etc. However, school does teach you about embarrassment and failure... and comparisons based on what you have or do not have. That can determine your popularity and chart the course for your level of confidence as you enter the adult world. But, no matter, my shoes were not helping.

Back on track here, here are some of the impacts of comparisons:

First, comparisons create dissatisfaction. You can always find someone prettier, thinner, more intelligent, more skilled, more accomplished, or with more possessions, connections, or success than you.

The acceleration of social media ramped up the tendency to make comparisons. What you see in others is what they want you to see, but not always the truth. Public persona and private reality are often vastly different. And comparisons are not always equal. Someone may seem hugely successful while privately struggling with addiction or depression. Perhaps, this is why we are so surprised when we see celebrities commit suicide. They are often unfairly judged, as people link their money to happiness.

Chasing comparisons can become a never-ending downward spiral, so be careful about your goals. What others portray may not be what it appears to be, and you may be doing yourself a grave disservice.

Second, comparisons also kill your self-esteem. Comparing yourself to others diminishes how you view yourself. It is easy to focus on the positives in everyone else while highlighting the negatives in yourself. Do yourself a favor; remember your talents instead of focusing on your flaws. There are enough critics who will constantly judge you; do not criticize yourself.

I remember a day when I was talking with a young, well-dressed, well-groomed woman who was lamenting certain aspects of her life. Her external image was almost flawless. She revealed that she was unhappy with her material and social status as she spoke. She consistently compared her possessions to those of several of her friends. She believed that she had not gotten her fair share.

After I departed from her, I mentally revisited our conversation. I also reflected upon dialogue with others in which I had noted a similar vein. The discourse of comparison is a common disorder of life. It creates the belief that someone else has the lion's share of the luck.

As you make comparisons, you are essentially judging others. There could be, and more than likely are, other hardships the person has endured to get where they are that are not obvious to you. Perhaps, more damaging, you may begin to make changes to emulate those you admire or envy. You may literally be headed toward mediocrity. And no, it is not about believing that you are better than others either, but thinking you are inferior to others limits your potential.

Third, there are a pair of comparisons to compare- intentional alliteration. Two that I feel are important to identify and determine if they are happening in your life are downward and upward comparisons:

People use downward comparisons when they feel bad and want to remind themselves that things could be worse. For example, when you have had a difficult day, you may tell yourself someone else has had a worse day. It is a way to boost confidence or self-esteem when either may have been damagaed. In some ways, this type of comparison helps you to see the bigger picture and may help you to have more compassion for others.

It is also easy to use others as your yardstick for self-elevation. When you measure yourself against those you feel superior to, you often use an inaccurate barometer.

If you repeatedly make downward comparisons, you are only building yourself up based on the misfortune of others. As a result, your self-esteem is precariously balanced. If you focus on downward comparisons, you are waiting for the next casualty to feel good.

Downward comparisons do not focus on your own personal strengths, positives, and successes. Instead, they merely focus on the downfall of others.

When the effectiveness of downward comparisons wears off, you could be left with scarred self-esteem. This could also lead to the belief that this is as good as you deserve for things to be... so be careful.

There is also the trapping of upward comparisons. This is where you focus on the strengths and successes of someone else. Then, you compare yourself to someone you perceive to be better off. Upward comparisons can help us meet our goals and motivate us to get where we want.

More often than not, however, upward comparisons can cause issues such as jealousy, envy, and low self-esteem. We create unrealistic standards for ourselves, which are unlikely to be healthy or sustainable choices, even if we try to achieve them.

Whichever comparison you make, it is wise to recognize it as merely a matter of perspective. The image you have of others is just one view. Everyone's lives are so much more complex than what they might portray.

It would be best if you also remembered that comparisons are not equal. So, you may think that someone has a better car, a fitter physique, or more money than you. But this does not mean that it is an accurate comparison or that their life is better than yours. Again, many people will try to portray 'perfection,' especially on social media. However, this is often nothing more than an illusion. You do not know how many times someone had failed before they were successful. You also do not know what that person is envious of. It may well be the attributes that you have.

It is great if your comparisons motivate you to adopt healthy lifestyle choices. However, if they make you unhappy and dissatisfied with yourself, it is time to switch off and focus on the most critical person... you.

Fourth, and perhaps most critically, comparisons can ruin friendships.

We should be supporting our friends with every single venture. However, we often use our friends to benchmark our lives and evaluate ourselves. Your friend may seem to have it all sorted with marriage and children. However, they could be envious of you for being free and able to travel and have adventures without as many commitments.

When we compare with friends, the friendship can become strained as you become rivals. A friend should not be someone you want to beat. They should be someone you want to build up. So, if you feel envious of what they have, remember things have a habit of evening out. Things that seem unbalanced will usually switch. Furthermore, with friends' successes, they may enable you to reach yours.

Hopefully, you will be able to see the positive changes you have made as your life progresses. If you must compare yourself to anyone, compare yourself to yourself from yesterday, last month, or last year. If you are better than you were in the past, give yourself credit.

This is not all mental, either. This is about your physical comparisons as well. If you worry that you used to be able to run a marathon with ease but now you are struggling with the weekly park run, think about the things that have changed in your life. Perhaps you have more stress, are not sleeping well, or are not devoting enough time to exercise.

Remember, it is impossible to compare accurately with anyone... sometimes even with yourself.

When you are solely looking at yourself for answers rather than what someone else is doing, you can remove any obstacle. You can then focus on the goals you want to achieve.

So, a key takeaway from this chapter- spend less time focusing on others- it often breeds mediocrity in your own life; it is time to focus on being your best and caring for yourself.

Self-care will be essential to breaking free from comparisons; caring more, in general, could lift you to heights you never dreamed of.

CHAPTER 5

Care More

To care more is in direct conflict with indifference... and that is a good thing.

In fact, it has been a rare occasion that I have met someone who cares deeply about what they do and delivers mediocre results. If they were mediocre from a results perspective, it was likely because they had reached their talent limit. See "The Peter Principle" I referenced earlier in the book.

Let me start by sharing a story:

I attended an offsite meeting in Seattle a few years ago while working for Starbucks. We were planning for the next fiscal year and decided to avoid the distractions of being in the middle of the action in the Starbucks headquarters called the Seattle Support Center, or SSC for short.

The SSC was the paragon of corporate energy- the constant

shuffling from meeting to meeting, the energy from the Starbucks store at the base of the building at that time, and the Third Place feel of the Starbucks store on the eighth floor. If you wanted connection, the SSC was the place.

However, if you wanted to focus, you needed to get out of the building, especially for something as important as strategic planning.

So, off we went to downtown Seattle.

There were two memorable moments from that offsite meeting.

First, we had planned this offsite meeting with outside consultants who had effectively built three days of content they were attempting to cover in two days- typical of consultants. I know, unnecessary cynicism, but not totally untrue.

This strategic plan would guide our work for the next year and beyond, so the importance of the meeting could not be overstated.

Knowing that we were working against an unreasonably limited amount of time, the consultants did the obvious thing that anyone would do given the circumstances- when we opened the meeting on the first day, they jumped right into the agenda. However, this was Starbucks- traditions and culture matter.

What tradition, what culture, you ask? Well, beginning all meetings with a coffee tasting.

Of course, there was no way the consultants could have known of this ritual- our responsibility was to educate them. So, I slowly raised my hand to not abruptly interrupt their opening salvo, but interrupt it, nonetheless. I politely provided the context and purpose of a coffee tasting at Starbucks and the tone that was set by opening each meeting with this ritual. Ritual seems so tribal, so primitive, so cult-like. Well, I _am_ describing Starbucks.

I must admit, I was surprised by the consultant's initial response. The consultants had courage; I will give them that. This was a Starbucks meeting, and now, with this full cultural knowledge disclosed, they were bold enough to say aloud that we did not have time for a coffee tasting. I mean, a conscious effort to open an off-cycle, strategy-setting Starbucks meeting without a coffee tasting- that was bold- bolder than the cup of Italian Roast that I had already consumed on my way to the meeting that morning.

I looked around the room as this proclamation was being made to gauge the reaction of the other participants. The tension in the room was palpable, but without my intervention, we were apparently going to kick off the meeting content without the coffee tasting.

I even had a moment of contemplation- was I overreacting? I thought about it and said no, I was not. A coffee tasting must occur. The good news is that the executive in charge of the meeting, Chris Carr, and the rest of the room agreed with this direction in an I-am-glad-someone-else-said-it-so-I-did-not-have-to way.

Nonetheless, since I was the one that interrupted the flow of the meeting, I felt inclined to lead the coffee tasting. Of course, no one said I had to, but no one else volunteered either, placing the responsibility at my feet.

No problem. I asked what coffee was brewed that had been placed in the back corner of the room. The local leader attending the meeting said it was Guatemala Antigua.

Ah, one of my all-time favorite coffees and a favorite of many Starbucks partners. Antigua is a unique coffee-growing region for Starbucks. At one point in their history, almost a third of all Starbucks coffee in the world was purchased from that one small region- that is how special Antigua is.

This revered coffee is grown near a volcano... and no ordinary volcano. Volcan de Agua is a perfectly shaped conical volcano that dominates the skyline of Antigua, Guatemala. It is a Holocene stratovolcano that has not erupted in historical times, considered the last five hundred years. The summit crater can be reached in a 4-5 hour walk up the steep slope from the Maya village of Santa Maria de Jesus. Sorry, I am having a flashback to what it was like to lead a coffee tasting. This is the level of research and insight that would be shared to educate others about the journey of coffee and the story of the farmers who cultivated the coffee.

Yes, at Starbucks, it is more than just tasting coffee. It is the story behind the coffee- the region, the coffee profile, the farmer stories.

Without prompting, one of the other senior leaders recognized the support needed for a coffee tasting and quickly shuffled to the back of the room and began to pour coffee.

As she walked around and began to serve the coffee, I pulled out my coffee passport and led the tasting for this special coffee. The coffee passport was a book used to capture our experiences every time we tasted coffee. At that time, I had participated in more than 1,000 coffee tastings- each a unique experience with Starbucks partners worldwide. I realized that I had documented fifty-six coffee tastings with this coffee alone- again, that is how special Guatemala Antigua is.

The memory of who you tasted the coffee with and what food you paired the coffee with were staples of a coffee passport entry. So, yes, food gets paired with coffee for tastings in much the same way as food is paired with wine.

So, back to the coffee tasting: I followed all the required steps- smell, slurp, locate, and describe. Through the process, we encourage participants to smell the coffee to share the aroma they are experiencing. I know I sound like a coffee elitist but stay with me. We then slurp the coffee to spray it across our palette. This is helpful because the coffee is usually tasted at scorching temperatures. Tasting coffee after it has cooled down can dramatically change the taste profile, so hot is preferred. Slurping helps to distribute the coffee without burning your tongue. Next, we locate- this describes where the coffee is most dominant on your palette. Wherever the coffee is more prevalent, your palette gives clues to the region where the coffee is grown. And finally, we describe the taste of the coffee. Coffee can taste nutty, like cocoa, like berries, etc. I know; now I really do sound like a coffee elitist.

The coffee demanded this type of detail... and reverence. This is important to share because of what comes next... storytelling.

I took the time to share some of the most memorable coffee experiences I had with this coffee over the years.

This description of coffee tastings is essential because of the love and care farmers pour into harvesting coffee. I will digress one more level to talk about coffee farmers. If ever there was an example of caring more, it is the story of coffee farmers.

Many farmers that Starbucks purchased coffee from own two hectares or less. The annual crop of coffee harvested, and the amount of income gained, based on a fair price offered, literally keeps thousands of families financially viable each year. The farmers love the coffee, but they also need the coffee.

Can I stop here and talk about a coffee experience with coffee farmers? This chapter is about caring more.

I traveled to Costa Rica a few years ago to spend time on a coffee farm. It was five amazing days in one of the true gems of Central America.

I developed such a deep appreciation for Costa Rica, and not just because of the country's beauty. It was more about the openness and acceptance, and foresight. For example, one notable fact is the Costa Rican Military has been gone for almost 75 years. The country has existed in peace despite civil wars and other conflicts experienced by most of it's neighbors.

The absence of an army makes it possible each year to fund all the country's public universities, leading to one of the highest literacy rates in the world.

Back to the coffee... On my first day in Costa Rica, I was knee-deep in coffee cherry. If you did not know, coffee grows on trees... seriously. Oh, so much to say, but let me stay on course with what is relevant here.

Being on the bed of a truck full of coffee, with all the vibrant colors of the rainbow, shoveling bushels of coffee to the coffee farmers waiting on the ground was as surreal as any experience I had with coffee. At that point, I had already spent eight years working for Starbucks, describing coffee to others as though I had a deep understanding of coffee. But, as it turns out, I had no idea what I was talking about until I arrived in Costa Rica.

Okay, back to the coffee tasting. The real gift from the coffee tasting that morning had nothing to do with me- of course, I did my best to honor the coffee. The real gift came from one of the other leaders in the room, Ricardo, who happened to oversee the Latin American region for Starbucks. I could see Ricardo's eyes light up when I began the coffee tasting, but I did not realize that Ricardo's excitement was because he had a story to tell.

As I concluded, Ricardo interjected and shared with the room that we would open our very first Starbucks store in the Antigua region in two weeks! That news took the room by surprise. I sensed two emotions- surprise that we were opening our first store there and no one in the room knew about it, and disappointment that we were opening our first store in the Guatemala Antigua region, and no one in the room knew about it.

Let me go to the top level of this.

Coffee tastings at Starbucks were everything at that time- as crucial to the culture as any other ritual. So, you may wonder what makes us care so much about coffee. Because it was who Starbucks was before all the drive-thru locations, blended drinks, and social media beverages. It was a humble little coffee shop that sold whole bean and ground coffee.

Overall, an interesting start to the day for sure.

The other memorable moment that day was meeting in the building where Howard Behar lived. Who is Howard Behar? Well, let me digress for a moment here too.

If you have read my other books, you may note that I rarely call any person by name, and those I do, are often fictitious names- that is intentional. However, there are times when I will break from that approach... and this is one of those occasions.

Howard Behar is as important to the Starbucks legacy as Howard Schultz. Howard Schultz may be the heart of Starbucks, but Howard Behar is not far behind. Howard Behar was the culture of Starbucks, the reason for Servant Leadership. In the days when all the critical decisions were being made that represent the Starbucks we know today, both Howards were there... every step of the way. Howard Behar was so important to Starbucks that when he left Starbucks, it never left him. He remained a brand ambassador.

More recently, Howard Behar came to speak at a franchise conference for Jamba Juice- I was the Chief Operating Officer then. The CEO and I shared an overlapping Starbucks history. As we were planning the meeting, the one person that we both thought about to inspire the audience of franchise owners and our leadership team was Howard Behar.

A call was set up to discuss the conference. A week later, the CEO and I were having a three-way conversation with Howard about the state of the business and the messaging that we believed he could interject into our event.

As the discussion unfolded, Howard's message began to come into view- it sounded a lot like Servant Leadership. This was important because one of the critical collective opportunities amongst the franchisees was to drive engagement in their employee ranks.

In true servant-leader fashion, Howard did not want to stand up and lecture the franchisees about how to lead. Instead, Howard wanted to have a conversation- so we did.

The CEO deferred to me to be the person on stage to have this conversation with Howard. I felt it was a great exchange back and forth. I had plenty of questions prepared for the session, but

I only got to ask a few as Howard's ability to tell a story was as strong as ever on that day. He provided just the right inspiration for the franchisees.

That is Howard Behar— every day.

So, when Howard walked into our downtown Seattle strategy meeting unannounced, it was pretty amazing.

With a surprised look on his face, Howard posed the question, "What are all of you doing here?" A couple of people responded with the intent of the meeting.

Chris Carr responded with a question of his own back to Howard, "What are you doing here?"

Howard quickly quipped, "I live here!"

Howard's response drew laughter from the room. What a coincidence we were meeting in the building where he resided... and what a treat.

I could see the discontent of the time-bound consultants who could feel their meeting agenda being highjacked again... and we were not yet at lunchtime on the first day. Although I believe it was beginning to become apparent, even to the consultants, of the significance of our unexpected guest.

Of course, we were behind on our agenda because of my righteous and impromptu coffee tasting that morning.

Nonetheless, Howard now had the floor.

Chris took the opportunity to fold Howard's presence into our agenda. While we were planning for the future, Chris believed that Howard's current day insight could help us.

While Howard has long since retired from Starbucks, he does take the time to visit Starbucks locations on his travels and often provides insight back to key leaders.

On this day, Chris wanted that feedback directly, particularly related to licensed store locations. So, Chris asked Howard, "What would you have us tell our license partners about maintaining and enhancing the brand?"

With conviction and without hesitation, Howard replied, "Care more."

It seems like a simple enough answer and certainly simple enough to execute. And yet, I thought- this was Howard's wisdom to impose upon this group? That is all? Two words?

I will not say that the impact was like Ralphie in A Christmas Story movie learning that the decoder led him to the secret of "Eat Your Ovaltine." Oh, I hope you have seen this movie before reading this. If not, my spoiler will leave you deeply disappointed at this emotional letdown during the movie.

Honestly, I just expected more. But, on reflection, that is not on Howard; that is on me and anyone else in the room that may have been experiencing the feelings that I was experiencing.

It was a stark reminder, and a lesson, that the simplicity of leadership always comes through, and this was that. Howard has been a master of leadership for decades, and this was his message.

My takeaway is that I often interact with leaders who have long speeches and presentations and, at the end of it all, do not deliver a clear message. Simplicity always helps to drive the message home. Simplicity also ensures that you have a message to drive home. Howard fully understood that at that moment.

This is where I tie the morning's activities to caring more and to indifference. Indifference would allow this meeting to occur without a coffee tasting. And then you look at all that would have been missed- the knowledge of the new store opening in Guatemala, the story of the coffee farmers, and the general connection over coffee. It would have been a fracturing of the culture at Starbucks. I know it may sound a bit melodramatic, but it is true. In fact, that is how culture is generally fractured in any company... one small act of indifference at a time. At the core of caring more is always leadership.

Speaking of leadership, a pivot here to another example of caring more.

There was an event from a few years ago that left a lasting impact on me. It was September 2015, when Pope Francis came to the United States.

Let me disclaim this by saying, and with no disrespect, that I am not a Catholic; it seems that everything these days must come with a disclaimer. However, this disclaimer is not for protection purposes. Instead, this demonstrates my respect for hearing something inspirational, something that makes sense, and something we can all apply to our daily lives, no matter what religion you subscribe to, if any at all. Even though I am not a Catholic, let me reference someone who is... John Boehner.

John Boehner, the former Speaker of the House, shocked the country when he announced his resignation from Congress in 2015. As you may recall, the historic visit of Pope Francis to the U.S. Capitol accelerated Boehner's decision to step down.

A Catholic who grew up one of twelve children, Boehner had worked for years to host the Pope at the U.S. Capitol. Finally, on September 24, 2015, his dream was realized when Pope Francis delivered the first-ever papal address to a joint session of Congress during his visit to the United States.

The image of Boehner trembling and crying as he met the Pope and while the Pope was addressing Congress is a moment that shook me emotionally. I suppose it was partly because members of Congress, in general, seem to be a group of emotionless people- I know that is not fair as we do not often get to see them in a personal or family setting. They should not necessarily come to work to cry every day. That said, when you care deeply about something, it can, and maybe should, move you to tears. I will come back to this point later.

To care more, you must have an authentic desire to serve others.

This is why the words of Pope Francis resonated so much with me. And not because he was the Pope but because he was human.

Before I get to the relevance of his trip to the United States, I want to recall some of the Pope's remarks from that historic day:

"Today, I would like not only to address you but through you, the entire people of the United States. Here, together with their representatives, I would like to take this opportunity to dialogue with the many thousands of people who strive each day to do an honest day's work, to bring home their daily bread, to save money, and – one step at a time – to build a better life for their families. These are people who are not concerned simply with paying their taxes but, in their own quiet way, sustain the life of society. They generate solidarity by their actions, and they create organizations which offer a helping hand to those most in need."

"Each son or daughter of a given country has a mission, a personal and social responsibility. Your own responsibility as members of Congress is to enable this country, by your legislative activity, to grow as a nation. You are the face of its people, their representatives. You are called to defend and preserve the dignity of your fellow citizens in the tireless and demanding pursuit of the common good, for this is the chief aim of all politics. A political society endures when it seeks, as a vocation, to satisfy common needs by stimulating the growth of all its members, especially those in situations of greater vulnerability or risk. Legislative activity is always based on care for the people. To this, you have been invited, called, and convened by those who elected you."

"All of us are quite aware of, and deeply worried by, the disturbing social and political situation of the world today. Our world is increasingly a place of violent conflict, hatred, and brutal atrocities."

"The challenges facing us today call for a renewal of that spirit of cooperation, which has accomplished so much good throughout the history of the United States. The complexity, the gravity, and the urgency of these challenges demand that we pool our resources and talents and resolve to support one another, with respect for our differences and our convictions of conscience."

"Politics is, instead, an expression of our compelling need to live as one, in order to build as one, the greatest common good: that of a community which sacrifices particular interests in order to share, in justice and peace, its goods, its interests, its social life. I do not underestimate the difficulty that this involves, but I encourage you in this effort. Here too, I think of the march which Martin Luther King led from Selma to Montgomery as part of the campaign to fulfill his "dream" of full civil and political rights for African Americans. That dream continues to inspire us all. I am happy that America continues to be, for many, a land of "dreams." Dreams which lead to action, to participation, to commitment. Dreams which awaken what is deepest and truest in the life of a people."

"Let us treat others with the same passion and compassion with which we want to be treated. Let us seek for others the same possibilities which we seek for ourselves. Let us help others to grow, as we would like to be helped ourselves. In a word, if we want security, let us give security; if we want life, let us give life; if we want opportunities, let us provide opportunities. The yardstick we use for others will be the yardstick which time will use for us."

Incredible words. Unfortunately, it left me contemplating a question that in and of itself is troubling to even ask, "Who talks like that anymore?"

We have seen a level of degradation in our communication, which has led to a lack of civility and an absence of hope in our communication. Obviously, not everyone, not everywhere, but on display often enough to be concerning for sure. The Pope was not talking as a figurehead of the Catholic church but as a mere man with integrity, kindness, and the desire to do good.

All of this is great, but what was most memorable about this papal visit was not what the Pope said but what he did.

He demonstrated care. He did something that almost none of our U.S. congresspeople do- go and spend time with everyday citizens. Not when there is a camera present for a photo opportunity, not when it is time to campaign, and not when it is convenient. Just because.

Pope Francis kissed babies and blessed people from all social classes when visiting Pennsylvania and New York. Pope Francis also got out of his Popemobile in East Harlem and walked to greet the crowd. He showed no fear for his safety. He had a singular focus... and that was to show that he cared about people.

The level of respect that the Pope gained and the hope he instilled was already being washed away three months earlier by a descent down an elevator in New York, one that would sharply change the trajectory of our country as it relates to decency and civility.

Caring more is an intentional act. It creates emotion in others. A bit more storytelling here.

I worked with a long-tenured director, Marie, many years ago who had the misfortune of her birthday always falling on the day of an offsite meeting. Looking back, I learned that I had become a creature of habit in terms of scheduling meetings, and consequently, one of my annual meetings was blocked in the same week four years in a row... coinciding with her birthday. This meeting cadence was consistent with my predecessor in this role, so add another four years of birthday misalignment. To Marie's credit, she never complained about it, but there it was on my calendar. I could not pretend that I did not see it.

Finally, I decided to do something about it... in year eight.

However, I did not move the meeting. In the end, it was still more trouble to move the meeting as this week always allowed for maximum participation, the weather was always perfect, and it was off-season for business travel, so rates were cheaper.

After the meeting details were finalized, I had my administrative assistant reach out to Marie's husband, Louis. There was an opportunity to make this birthday memorable for Marie... and include Louis. I received confirmation from my administrative assistant the next day that Louis was in on our scheme.

As the timing worked out, Marie's birthday fell on the first day of the offsite meeting. So, during lunch on day one of the meeting, the team sang happy birthday to Marie and presented her with cards and a cake. Everything went as planned.

Next came the surprise. When the meeting ended on day one, I announced our plans for dinner along with transportation details. Those details did not include Marie. Marie looked at me with a puzzled look on her face. I shared that she had different dinner plans from the rest of the team.

At that moment, Marie's husband appeared... and it was a moment. Louis walked out and surprised Marie, and the tears began to flow. I also saw a look of relief on Marie's face. I can only imagine her conversations with her husband year after year about the business requirement to be gone every year on her birthday. Marie had always done it with a smile, but inside, the anguish had to build up more every year. Not this year.

And oh, Louis' travel expenses and dinner were on me.

That was the least that I could do. Marie had already dedicated more than twenty years of service in total to this company.

I must admit that it was gratifying to hear the story of their wonderful evening the next day.

The story's takeaway is not what I did or the fact that I did it. Anyone could have done it and done that. What is most important is the care.

The reality is that, for this to unfold, I had to think about how to make this birthday memorable for Marie.

It is like giving flowers to someone- it is not the flowers as much as the act. When people say, 'It is the thought that counts," that is true- you literally had to have spent time thinking about the person.

To do caring things is as premeditated as any action we can take as humans. I know, premeditated is a word almost always used in a negative manner- I choose to repurpose it here for something positive.

Speaking of flowers and of doing caring things.

A couple of years ago, on Mother's Day, my wife decided to take flowers, walk out to our local park, and give flowers to all the mothers who may not have received any flowers that day. The responses were filled with gratitude, especially for those who had a spouse who apparently forgot.

Talk about caring. My wife is the epitome of caring. She knows how difficult it is to be a mother, and then to do it and not receive gratitude for it is even more challenging... especially on Mother's Day. More on my wife in a moment.

Another story: A few years ago, I demonstrated another deliberate act of care- I decided to fly from Austin to Houston on the birthday of one of the leaders on my team, Tracy. The local team arranged for Tracy to be in one of our stores, so I knew exactly where to go.

Everything worked out from a timing perspective, and when I walked into the store, Tracy had a puzzled look on her face. The look of 'Why is he here?' and 'What did I do or what did I miss on the calendar?' Of course, I would quickly reveal my purpose for being there to relieve the anxiety that was building.

It was Tracy's birthday, and I came to give her a card, balloons, and a gift and mostly to say thank you. That was it. I immediately turned around, returned to the airport, got on a plane, and flew back to Austin. It was important that I showed her how much she mattered.

I know that we cannot always 'get on a plane' to prove that we care about someone, but there are a thousand acts of caring that we can execute every day.

Caring more is not a philosophy. It is literally taking action. Executing any level of care means that you thought about the person... and therein lies the positive impact.

However, even with these actions, I consider myself an amateur when it comes to caring more. We all can find our own way to demonstrate care- these are just two of my examples.

This is another reason I titled this chapter Care More, not just Care. All of us can demonstrate care, but to care more is reserved for the special few. Those who will always put others before themselves, even when they do not have to.

If they identify someone in need, their focus is all in. The only way for those who care more to not behave in this way is not to be present. When you care this deeply, there is simply no sign of indifference... and, to my earlier point, you are often brought to tears.

Back to my wife: she is the person in my life who cares more than anyone I know.

The bottom line is this: I have never met anyone who cares more for others than she does... and I know some amazing people who care deeply. I am serious about making this lofty assertion. My wife's kindness and care are not driven by a job or motivated by recognition.

Jokingly, I have said that she has an enlarged heart. No, not in some troublesome way like a heart defect. More in the way that the Grinch's heart is believed to be two sizes too small, my wife's heart is possibly two sizes bigger than average.

She is always looking out for less fortunate people because she was that person growing up. She had to fight for everything and endure extraordinary situations that would have broken the average person.

I recognize that no two mothers are the same, and of course, no two children are the same; However, the love and care our three children received is on the level with anyone else- I really believe that. That is all because of my wife.

Even our dogs lived a great life. Not just because of the ability to provide the best health care, clothes, and toys that sometimes made our kids envious, but also genuine care.

I cannot remember a day that our dogs did not smile at us- yes, dogs do smile, or at least our dogs knew how to smile. They knew how well they had it living with us, and that too was all because of my wife.

Back to care more. There is a point to be made that Care More can be a misleading term. The question has been brought up to me, "Care more than what?" My response has always been the same- we can always do more than whatever we are doing. There is simply no cap on care.

The reality is that caring more does not always have to be this go-out-of-your-way activity- it is often trivial things right in front of us. That said, stepping out and showing care in obvious and meaningful ways can change someone's life.

I watch how small children, who are total strangers, play together. When they see another toddler fall, they say uh-oh and go to help them stand up again.

I believe we are born with that kind spirit, which is chipped away as we grow. Some of us make it to adulthood with our caring nature intact. Most often, thanks to the ecosystem of people we are surrounded with, we do not make it that far. Many of us are tainted with evil and discourse from early in our lives. By adulthood, we have developed tendencies that are in direct conflict with caring.

We could show disdain for the world around us, and yet, there is that something we love that softens our hearts. That one thing... and that is all it takes. Kindness and caring are somewhere within each of us... they just need to be nurtured.

Speaking of kindness...

CHAPTER 6:

Respond With Kindness

I am following the last chapter with this topic of kindness because kindness is taking care to the next level.

Kindness also eliminates indifference. The act of being kind confirms to someone else that you are intentional about doing something nice for them, even when there is no motivation.

Indifference breeds the bystander mentality I spoke about earlier in the book. Kindness eliminates that. People that demonstrate kindness engage... they always engage.

While the opposite of kindness is, logically, being unkind, I think equally opposite is indifference.

None of the core behavior traits of kindness lend themselves to being indifferent. Some of those behavioral traits include good listening skills, social interaction, generosity, charity, helping, and being courteous.

One of my challenges in studying kindness lies in its different definitions.

Kindness is listed in the dictionary as a noun, but the way I see it, kindness is a verb. If nothing actionable happens, then kindness does not occur. Kindness must manifest itself into a demonstrated behavior.

One definition states that kindness is a behavior marked by ethical characteristics, a pleasant disposition, and concern for others.

Kindness is more than definitions- it is action. We are also learning that kindness can be quantified in its impact.

Researchers from KindLab at Kindness.org conducted a meta-analysis of twenty-seven experiences. Here are a few of their findings:

• Kindness ranked above physical attractiveness in selecting a potential mate.
• If a doctor expressed kindness, surveyed patients who had a cold recovered a day faster than normal.
• Kindness can lower the effects of stress.
• Being kind to others boosts psychological flourishing.
• Kindness is an effective way to reduce social anxiety.

Richard Ryan & Edward Deci, two psychology professors, wrote about the topic of kindness back in 2001. They concluded that happiness can be measured. They also measured gratitude as it related to participants' response to receiving kindness.

Here are some of their findings:

- Happy people scored higher on their motivation to perform and their recognition and enactment of kind behaviors.
- Happy people have more happy memories in daily life in terms of both quantity and quality.
- Subjective happiness was increased simply by counting one's own acts of kindness for one week.
- Happy people became more kind and more grateful through kindness encounters.
- People with less money show more generosity, charitability, and helpfulness.
- Children who are more socially active exhibit more prosocial behavior.
- Kindness is positively related to better self-regulation and less emotional reactivity.

That said, finding a scientifically validated list of what it takes to be a kind person does not exist. However, in multiple studies, the same traits continued to surface.

Have you ever been in line at a coffee shop and been surprised when the barista tells you your order was paid for by a stranger in front of you?

You then decide to pay for the person behind you. These are often called "Random Acts of Kindness." In actuality, there is nothing random about it. People are intentionally kind.

Kindness has been proven to be highly contagious in multiple studies throughout the years. In a study conducted back in the

1960s, passing drivers witnessed a woman standing beside a car with a flat tire. One-half of the passing drivers had previously witnessed a staged setting of a man helping a woman in a comparable situation; the other half of drivers had not.

Researchers found that the motorists who had witnessed the staged kind act beforehand were significantly more likely to stop and help the woman.

Let me further amplify the significance of the word kindness.

For starters, kindness is one of the most difficult words to hijack with an alternate narrative. Let me explain:

There are powerful words in the English language, like love. In fact, it is hard to argue that there is a stronger word than love, kindness included. However, love can be highjacked. You can love things that are not good for your health, like cake and pizza. You can also love things that are not universally loved, like hunting or stealing. Love can even turn into obsession-unhealthy love.

Kindness, though, is incredibly difficult to hijack. I will go as far as to say that you cannot turn kindness into a negative narrative. When you say kindness, everyone immediately knows what it is and is not. Kindness is not just about being nice instead of being mean. It is also being nice in the face of meanness.

So, what does kindness really look like?

I believe that kindness is a compilation of four qualities, three of which are interconnected- Empathy, Compassion, and Sympathy. The fourth quality is Forgiveness. I will come back to the last one shortly.

Here is a short story that illustrates the definition of kindness.

A farmer had puppies he needed to sell. He painted a sign advertising the four pups and set about nailing it to a post on the edge of his yard. As he drove the last nail into the post, he felt a tug on his overalls. He looked down into the eyes of a little boy.

"Mister," he said, "I want to buy one of your puppies."

"Well," said the farmer, as he rubbed the sweat off the back of his neck, "These puppies come from fine parents and cost a good deal of money."

The boy dropped his head for a moment. Then reaching deep into his pocket, he pulled out a handful of change and held it up to the farmer. "I have thirty-nine cents. Is that enough to take a look?"

"Sure," said the farmer. And with that, he let out a whistle. "Here, Dolly!" he called.

Out of the doghouse and down the ramp ran Dolly followed by four little balls of fur. The little boy pressed his face against the chain link fence. His eyes danced with delight. As the dogs made their way to the fence, the little boy noticed something else stirring just inside the doghouse. Slowly another little ball appeared, this one noticeably smaller. Down the ramp, it slid.

Then in an awkward manner, the littlest pup began hobbling toward the others, doing its best to catch up.

"I want that one," the little boy said, pointing to the runt. The farmer knelt down at the boy's side and said, "Son, you do not want that puppy. He will never be able to run and play with you like these other dogs would."

With that, the little boy stepped back from the fence, reached down, and began rolling up one leg of his trousers. In doing so, he revealed a steel brace running down both sides of his leg, attaching itself to a specially made shoe. Looking back up at the farmer, he said, "You see, sir, I don't run too well myself, and he will need someone who understands."

With tears in his eyes, the farmer reached down and picked up the pup and handed it to the little boy.

This is kindness personified. The little boy felt sympathy for the runt of the litter but also empathy as he could relate to what the puppy would face in its life. His compassion caused him to act on what he was feeling.

Back to the fourth quality of kindness- forgiveness. Forgiving may be the single most challenging thing to do in life. It may also be the most important of the four pillars representing the practice of kindness.

The act of forgiveness. It means that something has gone wrong, and perhaps the only way to correct it is to swallow your pride and do something against your so-called "better judgment."

Forgiveness played a significant role in my journey of processing the deaths of both of my parents.

In the past few years, I lost both my mother and my father. Waking up without either parent in my life every day is a very sobering feeling. I do not wish it on anyone. Nonetheless, I am left to carry on.

My mother experienced a lot of physical suffering in her final years of life that only intensified the closer she got to death. For a woman in perfect health for the first seventy years of her life, the last five years, until her passing, were a struggle. Every time I visited her, I wanted to feel something different; I wanted to feel encouraged and to help her feel encouraged. However, my frustration would take over as I wrestled with her physical deterioration. Not my proudest moments. I share this as I suspect someone reading this has had to manage a complicated relationship with a parent at the end of life.

I use the word frustration because my mother was sometimes challenging to get along with. She was the quintessential glass-half-empty person with most aspects of her life, almost always emphasizing the worst in people. I never really understood that part of her, but it often put us at odds because of my belief that we should demonstrate kindness towards everyone all the time.

I wish I could tell you I was strong during her declining health, but I was not. I would visit her at the nursing home and then sit in my car and cry. It was a deep pain that will stay with me forever.

One visit, in particular, has lingered with me. It was about six months before my mother passed away. The disease she contracted took all her motor skills and, ultimately, even her motor skills of speaking. There were only whisperers and shallow breathing for months as her eyes told me she wanted to say something, but her mouth would no longer cooperate. However, there was this moment, after her voice was completely gone for weeks, when she looked at me with a look that I had not seen before and said, "Help me."

I was paralyzed. I have never been so uncertain in all my life about what to do with two simple words. I could not tell her I could not help her, but my eyes told her I could not help her. It was the level of hopelessness in her eyes that gave the words even more meaning.

Any frustration that I had experienced over the years slowly melted away as I could only have a forgiving heart for what she was experiencing. She had been such a strong and independent woman all her life that I did not recognize the person in the bed, slowly fading away.

In the subsequent months after my mother's passing, I did a lot of self-reflection. I was overcome with forgiveness. I began searching for the meaning of her life and retracing experiences that may validate her behavior when she was alive and what caused conflict in our relationship.

From an emotional support perspective, I felt that I completely failed my mother. Perhaps, if I had read to her more, comforted her more, or come to visit more often, it would have made a difference. These are the things that I tell myself. For that, I prayed for her forgiveness.

Forgiveness is such a powerful emotion that it can cause you to apologize for things you did not even do. Sometimes, you must step over the line and do more to mend a relationship for the person incapable of doing so on the other side.

I also had to walk through the journey of forgiveness recently when my father passed away... but for different reasons than my mother. I did not have a good understanding of my father's life and all the things he had gone through. However, in recent years we reconnected, and we were able to talk through those experiences. Each conversation made me look at his life differently, and it made his passing peaceful... for him and me.

I must admit, for years, my heart was hardened because of the absence of a relationship with my father. I was named after him, I looked just like him, and we did not have a relationship. His choice, not mine, or so I thought, for more than thirty-five years.

I saw my father intermittently over the years, but he appeared as a stranger across the room. It was a very confusing feeling. That, coupled with my attempts to connect with him over the years by calling him only to get nothing in return, only intensified the pain and, in some ways, pushed me further away. I could not understand how someone who raised me for the first few years of my life, before divorcing my mother, could show absolutely no interest in me. So, over time, any real interest in forming a relationship with him continued to wane. I suppose that you could say that I became indifferent. I knew I had a father and knew how to reach him, but he was unreachable.

And then, one day in early 2019, forgiveness entered the picture. I began to ask the 'what if' questions: what if this was all a big misunderstanding? What if he felt a level of guilt or embarrassment? What if it was simply that he was a man born in the late 1930s to an emotionally detached father who did not know how to show him love?

I suppose that enough of these questions began to assemble in a way that opened the door and moved me to action. At least, enough for me to make one more valiant effort for a connection... and so I did.

I called my father in January of 2019, and it changed everything. A few days later, I visited my father in Louisville, Kentucky; the rest was history. We rebuilt our relationship. We talked, we laughed, we connected. Of course, I cried, and I cried even more when he uttered those three most important words for the first time, "I love you." I cannot imagine what it took for him to say it, and then he kept saying it- every time I visited or we talked on the phone.

While I wrestled internally with the gap in time that could never be made up, the new connections began to ease the pain of the past. With each conversation, I gained an understanding of how he truly felt. There was no malicious intent in his lack of connection over the years. In fact, I did sense a level of guilt and embarrassment, which kept my father from reaching out when it seemed so obvious for him to do so.

I forgave my father. Not because I had to but because I wanted to. When my mother passed away, it was a very traumatic experience. I cried over her casket, I cried at the gravesite, and I cried for weeks and months. When my father passed away, it was a level of peace that I had never experienced before. I knew he had lived a full life, almost eighty-six years, and peacefully passed away in his apartment.

As I contrast the end of life for both my mother and father, all within a relatively brief period, I cannot help but reflect on the specific point that binds me to them- forgiveness.

So, kindness does not have to be a gesture of apparent goodwill, like helping someone with their groceries or allowing someone to cut in line in a rush. Kindness can be the emotional journey to show grace during adversity. Perhaps, even when you have the right to be mean or upset toward that person.

The relationship and conflict between kindness and indifference are real. Indifference can cause us to stay at a distance. Staying at a distance keeps us from feeling anything. Avoiding any feelings prevents empathy, sympathy, compassion, or forgiveness from entering the picture. That is how powerful indifference can be. Indifference keeps you safely "on the sidelines" of life.

I suppose some people will choose this "safety" in their life- to protect themselves and their own heart. And yet, the heart needs nourishment just like other parts of our body.

A quick story here to put a fine point on kindness:

A poor boy named Steve was selling goods door to door to pay for his studies. It was a difficult way to make ends meet, and one day, he found that he had only one dollar left and was hungry. While approaching the next house, he decided to ask for a meal.

But when a young woman opened the door, he lost his courage and could only dare to ask for a glass of water. The young woman looked at him and could see the desperation on the boy's face. So, instead of water, she brought him a plate of cookies and a large glass of milk. The boy drank the milk, ate the cookies, and then asked how much he owed her. The woman replied: "You do not owe me anything. Mother taught us never to accept pay for an act of kindness." The boy responded, "Then I thank you from the bottom of my heart." The boy's name was Steve Kelly.

Many years passed. One day that same woman became seriously ill. Local doctors could not help her. Therefore, they sent her to the big city, where specialists would study her rare disease. Dr. Steve Kelly was called in for the consultation. When he entered her room in the hospital, he immediately recognized the woman who showed him kindness when he was poor. The doctor was determined to do his best to help her recover from her disease.

The struggle was long, but together they managed to overcome her illness. A few months later, the woman received a bill for her treatment. She was worried that the amount to pay would be so significant that it would take the rest of her life to pay for it. Finally, when the woman opened the bill, she noticed words that were written on the side of the bill. The words were: "Paid in full with a plate of cookies and a glass of milk."

That is the power of kindness. Whether you believe in Karma, comeuppance, or something else spiritual, it is interesting to see this woman's kindness come full circle later in her life.

The best thing about kindness is that anyone can demonstrate it. Kindness will drive out indifference... it just will. Kindness is also so powerful that it can keep us from blaming others when things do not go our way. Without the presence of kindness, the blame game can rear its head.

CHAPTER 7:

The Blame Game

I will start here by restating a passage from earlier in the book:

"Doing nothing or wishing a problem away is a form of poor leadership. Playing it safe has never shown up as a strong leadership strategy. Staying silent is not a good look either."

Perhaps, the only trait more troubling than any of these for a leader is casting blame on others. Nothing says weak leadership like avoiding responsibility, especially when something goes wrong. Of course, taking credit for what you did not accomplish does not show up well either, but let's focus on blame.

Blaming someone else for something you had responsibility for or had the wherewithal and resources to do something about it and did not act, is mediocrity personified.

There are plenty of examples of the blame game that I will get into throughout this chapter.

I will start with this: I believe it would be irresponsible to author a book at this time in history, discuss the topic of blame, and not write about the Covid-19 pandemic. Well, I would skip the subject altogether... if things had gone well. But unfortunately, at the publishing of this book, I can report that things did not go well. In fact, it was much worse than any estimate at the beginning of the pandemic. For further emphasis, it is more than four years later, we are still dealing with the effects of the pandemic, and I am still discussing it.

There were plenty of examples of mediocrity and indifference during the pandemic, starting with a little thing called face masks. Sigh...

The politicization of face masks put a lot of people at risk and ultimately contributed to unnecessary deaths- unnecessary, given that none of us knew anything about this disease. I know, there is a faction who will say, "Covid did not kill people; it was their pre-existing condition that killed them." You know, the condition they were living with just fine before Covid came along? That one? Boy, a mask certainly would have helped. I heard that the fitment of a face mask was much better than that of a mask from a ventilator. Yes, I am dripping with sarcasm, but I am choosing this route to cover up my deep sadness.

The indifference, the lack of care, and the "I Didn't Know" posturing were all present to help drive the animosity towards the most basic of safety procedures- wear a mask. That, along with washing your hands and getting vaccinated. An open book test to survival that we failed miserably. At the printing of this book, and to be balanced in the conversation here, plenty of published studies showed that the vaccinations did little to protect people in the ways we communicated, even though fewer vaccinated people per capita died from Covid compared to unvaccinated people. To be fair, those studies could be wrong too. What is not disputable is that projected saliva, a part of all our everyday conversations, cannot be transmitted from one person to another if both people wear a mask- it just cannot happen. I get it, it is possible at 0.001%. That said, if you wore the mask below your chin or your nose hung out, all bets were off. Thousands failed the open book test of properly strapping on a simple face mask.

I cannot put the rejection of masks on any one person except to say this: when you are in a leadership role, you should act like a leader.

For any leader, at any level, who publicly stood at a podium and declared that they do not wear a mask, that they just do not like them, immediately parted the sea, and created a political riff. Beyond that, it emboldened everyday people to take that same brazen stance without any factual information and, maybe most important, without access to the same medicines that rich and powerful people had access to. Subsequently, deaths ensued.

Being on a ventilator in a hospital room or hallway, taking your final breaths, and still proclaiming that it is a hoax and you do not have Covid was not a good look. Well, actually, it was worse than that- it was deadly.

Going up to 50,000 feet on the pandemic, the blatant disregard for how the virus came to be in the United States, and the grave risk of calling it a virus named after Asian culture was grossly irresponsible. I mean, where do I even start with this? Well, hundreds of Asian Americans died in our country in the past few years due to hate crimes generated by the irresponsibility of those using virus labels. The conspiracy theories of Asian countries intentionally bringing the virus to the United States did not help either. Again, to be balanced, I will not dispute those who have purported proof that the coronavirus started in Wuhan- that very well may be true.

This is where placing blame becomes a serious matter. From there, we collectively did not do much to keep the coronavirus from getting from Wuhan to our shores.

What am I referring to? The panicked public announcement that sent thousands of Americans scurrying back to our country, flooding U.S. airports. You remember the images. By the way, none of the passengers were tested, and none of them were quarantined, just released into the wild, potentially going home and infecting their families, friends, and co-workers at a far more alarming rate than any other method of transmission at that time.

And then there were the cruise ships. Instead of resolving the issue at sea, in a truly quarantined environment, we also decided to release that group into the wild. Coming to port and quarantining for 14 days and then being released when we knew nothing more 14 days later is basically the same as releasing the airport passengers immediately.

You may be reading this attempting to determine what "side" I am on. My side is the side of decency, civility, care, and hope... oh, and common sense. You can decide what that means. The point here is that Covid should not have been partisan. It was a human health crisis... all humans were at risk.

If you remember that moment, blame was being placed everywhere as the virus began to rage out of control. I get it; none of this matters if you believe it was a hoax... but let me push on.

Then there was the Clorox incident with the good doctor. She was silent in arguably her most defining career moment- at least from a public perspective. She was the person who could have stopped the nonsense about ingesting Clorox. Some may say it was a lack of courage. Sure, it was, but it was also a form of indifference by staying silent. Those things you are genuinely passionate about will not allow you to be quiet... ever.

That moment had the makings of a turning point- a return to reason, logic, science, and then... nothing. It did not have to be a public admonishment; it just had to be the mention of 'Hey, do not drink Clorox.' Even Clorox passed on the burgeoning sales opportunity and denounced the incident. That was also an open-book test, and the good doctor failed. I am using this incident because it is essential to recognize indifference. To be fair, in the aftermath of that moment, you could no longer hold accountable the person making the comment about Clorox. In his defense, he even looked over to her for alignment and confirmation of his suggestion, and she stayed silent. Everyone has heard the moniker that silence is consent. Well, this was that.

The responsibility, and by proxy, the blame shifted to the doctor. I know this is a harsh stance, but I am attempting to trace back to how we get to some of the life situations that occur. So often, if we do not recognize and identify what happened, the probability of it happening again can and likely will happen. Leadership is not easy- if it were, everyone would do it, and everyone would do it well.

In our professions, we study, practice, and train for these moments- whether it is an attorney with a high-profile trial, or a surgeon performing a life-saving surgery, we are expected to put all our experience to work. She did not.

The pandemic created an environment that tested all leadership. In fact, you may have heard this quote before, "Crisis doesn't create character; it reveals it." I am not asserting that leadership was easy during a situation like a global pandemic that did not have a playbook; however, I urge people not to step into a leadership role if you do not believe that you can come through when adversity arrives.

It may appear that I am attacking only certain leaders. Our head of the National Institute of Allergy and Infectious Diseases misled us and made many missteps along the way too, as well as the current administration. Believe me; there was enough blame to go around- up, down, and across all levels and through all parties and all types of leadership. Some were simply more costly than others.

Again, there were significant leadership gaps related to Covid in all states, agencies, and levels. The reality is there were hundreds of opportunities to fix mistakes related to Covid... it is called tomorrow. And yet, day after day, we failed repeatedly, misinforming the public, misleading them, and ultimately forcing Americans to take sides, which led to some taking the side of death—a harsh lesson for sure. Blame was at the core of countless acts of indecision or inaction.

I mean, really, blaming someone for your indecision, inaction, or indifference is as troublesome as apologizing to someone, but while you are saying you are sorry, you are also explaining why you did it, whatever it is. That just does not work.

The blame game is a real thing, and it is a real problem. It is a problem because it creates a direct line to indifference and mediocrity, and it sets the table for a lack of trust and lack of other virtues that, when absent, erode personal or professional relationships.

There are plenty of examples of the blame game that have nothing to do with the pandemic.

And then there was the general.

You cannot forget what happened at Lafayette Square. By the way, the general was wearing combat fatigues. If there was any doubt about whether he was "on the clock," this certainly answered that.

While everyone lauded the general's apology, exceptionally

long after the event, for appearing during this incident near the White House after authorities forcibly removed peaceful protesters from the area, I had a completely different take on it.

First, remember this is American soil, these are American citizens, and these are American citizens exercising their right to protest... peacefully. Throwing tear gas and using force to disperse the "angry mob" is unacceptable on so many levels. Did I mention that the general was wearing combat fatigues?

An apology should never be dismissed, but leadership is not just about doing the right thing but also the right thing at the right time. Leadership is about the moment of truth.

Standing in a dark gym long after a basketball game is over and making the two free throws you needed to make an hour earlier to win the game when the arena was full of 10,000 screaming fans does not matter. No one cares afterward. This is the harshness of leadership and performance.

Did I mention that the general was wearing combat fatigues? I am not former military, but those who are in the military will tell you that was not acceptable. For me, the image of attacking our own citizens through military-backed action is a tough image to shake.

Tough talk, book tours, and speeches about what you did well feels a bit self-serving, but I also recognize those were extraordinary times. Again, this is why real leadership matters... really matters.

The blame game is just as prevalent in our personal lives. When we get a speeding ticket, we want to take our anger out on the police officer. We immediately offer an excuse, such as "I was going with the flow of traffic," blaming someone else, or "I didn't see the sign noting the speed change," blaming something else. We try to excuse our behavior and lessen the guilt and even the consequence of our sins. In this example, we almost always know that we are speeding. It is about as intentional of a violation that we commit in any part of our daily routine, and yet we still try to wiggle out of it by placing the blame somewhere else. We are just hoping that the police officer will not stop us and "bring us the news."

When we are late for work, we want to blame other drivers for not getting out of the way. When we are late paying a bill, somehow it is the creditor's fault.

Of course, the easy answer is that we should simply stop blaming others. It is not that easy, and yet, it is.

The truth is we do not like to admit when we are wrong, and when we are caught, we want to shift the blame to someone or something else.

Changing our course of action and avoiding the temptation of blaming others may not put us on the path to greatness, but it can at least divert us from the path of mediocrity.

Blame is happening in every facet of life, especially in business. But be careful; in a business setting, blame can be disguised.

Because collaboration is crucial to getting work done, it allows one collaborator to blame another, creating a different challenge- who to hold accountable.

The blame game in the work environment is literally an art form for some. Those struggling with work performance will often turn to blame, perhaps as a last resort, but turn to it, nonetheless. If the fear of losing their job is great enough, the blame card will get played- it is simply the human instinct of survival.

Let me shift and share this quick story I read recently:

A minor league baseball team manager had about all he could take. His team was getting blown out, and the lack of effort by his players reflected that. During one of the season's first games, the manager was so disgusted with his center fielder's performance that he ordered him to the dugout, and the manager assumed the position himself. The first ball that came into the outfield took a bad hop and hit the manager squarely in the mouth. The next one was a high fly ball, which he lost in the sun's glare allowing it to bounce off his forehead. The third was a line drive that he charged aggressively; unfortunately, it flew between his hands and smacked him directly in the eye. Furious, the manager ran back to the dugout, grabbed the center fielder by the uniform, and shouted. "You idiot! You have the outfield so messed up that even I cannot do a thing with it!"

Wow! Funny yet laced with a level of truth about what happens when we let our emotions get the best of us and blame others.

We hear stories all the time about people blaming others, even bringing frivolous lawsuits. Some are so ridiculous that they cannot be believed, but they end up on the docket in a real court before a real judge. Unfortunately, these stories often occur with everyday activities like:

If someone cuts a finger off while slicing salami at work, they blame the faulty equipment.

If someone smokes three packs of cigarettes a day for forty years and dies of lung cancer, their family blames the tobacco company.

If someone crashes into a tree while driving home drunk, they blame the alcohol maker.

Unfortunately, there are real cases involving each of these three examples.

Blame also shows up in behavioral ways too. Think about some of the rationalizations that occur when we are dealing with a difficult situation. Here are a few:

When the other person takes a long time, he is slow; when I take a long time, I am thorough.

When the other person does not complete a task, she is lazy; when I do not complete a task, I am busy.

When the other person does something without being told, he is overstepping his bounds; when I do it, that's initiative.

When the other person overlooks an etiquette rule, she is rude; when I skip a few rules, I am original.

You see where I am going here.

The blame game requires an introspective look at your own life and your approach to the environment around you.

Everything you have in your life is a manifestation of how you treat yourself, not how somebody else treated you or what somebody else has done.

I hope you bookmark this next point, if bookmarking is still a thing.

Accepting responsibility is a passage to adulthood.

Again, this is not a self-help book; this is a self-reflection book. If everything I shared had been easy to do, you would have already done it.

We can get away with many things as children- blaming is one of them. But, unfortunately, blaming is not a winning position as an adult. Many young adults want to proclaim their adulthood all while holding their parents accountable for their shortcomings. You cannot have it both ways. No matter your age, you have not fully graduated to adulthood until you are admittedly fully accountable for all your actions and outcomes. This is a big statement, and one that I hope lingers with you for a moment.

So, yes, you could already be married, have children, and have an excellent job, but not be a fully functional adult. Okay, it is my opinion, but we would not need nearly as many counselors, psychiatrists, and psychologists if all adults took control and responsibility for their lives.

I get it. I can hear some of your responses: "You do not know what I have gone through," "There are some traumatic events I had to endure," and "My situation is unique." Yep, everybody has gone through something during childhood. I am being a borderline jerk right now... intentionally.

Blame opens the door to so many problems in our lives. This is why I cannot let you off the hook here. This probably feels personal, and it should.

Consider these examples: What if everyone took ownership when an auto accident occurred and admitted their fault? Or when someone is accused of a crime, they confess. Imagine even more accountability- the person committing a crime comes forward, even when no one knows they committed it.

Blaming others or making excuses for our behavior is a waste of time because no matter how much fault we find in others or blame someone else, it will not change us and certainly not add to our growth or success.

Instead of blaming others, we should focus on how to avoid shifting blame. Here are a few examples:

Take A Deep Breath. The active process of stopping to take a deep breath can be therapeutic. It can also keep you from reacting emotionally to a situation and inviting the temptation of casting blame on someone else.

I have heard leaders advise that when composing an angry text or email, step away from it before hitting send, launching blame into the universe. If you return to the message-in-waiting hours later and still feel the same emotion, it may be relevant enough to hit send and deal with the aftermath later. Otherwise, allow yourself a moment of reflection that a deep breath can create.

Finally, taking a deep breath allows for better decision-making in general. Pausing to consider other options is critical- like the one where you take ownership of the problem.

If You Shift The Blame, Apologize. This is a big one. Demonstrating wisdom by apologizing when you have made a mistake is a crucial tenet of leadership. Often, it is easier to simply mask the problem, especially if no one is aware of the circumstances or blame you have cast. However, the person that does know is likely the person who has been beaten up for your lack of courage to come forward.

But be careful. If you apologize too often, that is a sign of another problem. Making the same mistakes repeatedly and apologizing is effective for only so long. Apologies should be rare but appropriate when they are necessary.

And remember, a sincere apology does not include explaining why you did what you did. That will land you right back into the vicious cycle of blame.

Keep Things In Perspective. Perspective often runs alongside wisdom and vice versa. Perspective opens the door for real-time reflection and usually allows for a much more balanced approach to issues that arise. With perspective in place, you are less likely to assign blame.

If you just accept responsibility in the first place and move on, you will be all the better for it. Chances are you will imagine the consequences far worse than they will actually be.

The ultimate level of ownership is acknowledging somewhere along the way that your blaming behavior may be what is holding you back. The blame game may have also caused you to miss key details along the way. The attention to those details matter.

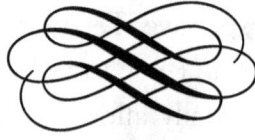

CHAPTER 8:

Attention To Detail

Mediocrity and indifference can cause many things to be missed—sometimes big things, sometimes small things, but often things that will matter later.

When things matter, we pay attention to all the little details. The same is true of leaders. Leaders that pay attention to detail signal that the person or task is important. Strong attention to detail leaders do not walk by the small things... ever. That means that indifference has no chance of existing in their space.

I will share stories about two very meticulous leaders I worked with that demonstrated the impact of paying attention to detail-two different leaders at two different companies at two different times of my life and career. Their attention to detail taught me much about caring and, as a result, drove away mediocrity and indifference as I developed my leadership footprint.

The first person is Nigel Travis. Nigel left an indelible mark on me at a pivotal time in my career. I was in a senior director role trying to break through to a vice-president position, and I had become a bit cynical about my future possibilities. I needed to see what was possible at the top of the food chain that could inspire me to push even harder. Nigel was that North Star.

Nigel was the most knowledgeable executive I had ever been around- then or since. Every morning was a challenge for Nigel to consume as much information as possible. He understood the value of current affairs and the impact that they could have on making decisions.

Nigel had spent time in fast food retail and a long stint in human resources before coming to Blockbuster, where we met.

When I arrived at the Blockbuster headquarters to work, Nigel was president of US retail. He was also responsible for the franchise side of the business, and after a year of working in the headquarters, I ended up in a franchise role, where I began to spend time with Nigel.

Before Blockbuster, I had never met an executive that demonstrated the level of care for people that I saw in Nigel. Perhaps, it was his earlier human resources experience. However, over time, I realized that was just who Nigel was- the HR job only enhanced what was a core attribute of his.

With all the business challenges we faced at Blockbuster in those days, I never saw Nigel rattled by new problems. Considering all the issues that presented themselves at Blockbuster, that is a strong statement. However, I believe nothing surprised Nigel because of his preparedness and attention to detail.

Nigel always solved problems through the lens of people... even during the most challenging times. In reflection, the level of care that Nigel demonstrated made a difference in our culture at the time. Many years and companies later, Nigel would author a book about culture. So, when I first saw his published book on the market, my initial response was, "That makes sense."

Nigel was so well-respected that there was a case to be made for Nigel becoming the CEO at Blockbuster. With no upward mobility based on the then-current CEO having such a firm grip on the role, that opportunity for Nigel never materialized.

Only a couple of short years later, it was not a surprise to see Nigel leave Blockbuster to take on the top job as CEO at Papa John's. The founder of Papa John's had success with the brand up until that time, but as with many founder-led companies, you can become limited in your thinking. There are many well-documented business case studies of a founder being able to grow a business to a certain point and then needing a new leader with a fresh perspective to continue the growth. It's just the evolution of business and best-in-class founders prepare for it.

For Papa John's, that leader was Nigel Travis. From a distance, I watched Nigel work, and I observed the level of success that he attained. Nigel cared deeply about the people and the brand-that is what you want and need from the person in the top job.

Nigel would ultimately leave the top job at Papa John's and take on the CEO job at Dunkin' Donuts. By then, I had moved on to Starbucks, so let the proverbial coffee wars begin.

I would always say to others at Starbucks, that while we are clearly the leader in the industry, this I know to be true: we should never fear our competitors, but we should always respect them. I would then use Dunkin' Donuts, specifically Nigel Travis, as an example. I knew firsthand of Nigel's attention to detail, and that behavior would permeate the new organization he was responsible for. Nigel had a vision to aggressively grow Dunkin' Donuts franchise locations, particularly in the Southern and Western parts of the country where the brand had little visibility. If anyone could pull it off, it would be Nigel Travis.

Of course, Dunkin' Donuts could not realistically challenge the size of Starbucks.

However, as is often said in a sports context, Nigel gave Dunkin' Donuts "the best chance to win." Nigel had much success as CEO there, which was no surprise to me. Nigel applied his philosophy of creating a challenge culture at every stop throughout his career but truly refined that principle at Dunkin' Donuts.

Allow me to go back and talk about this attention to detail that I saw in Nigel, up close and personal. The first time I met Nigel Travis was actually long before I went to work in the corporate ofice. It was 1999, and I was a brand-new regional director at Blockbuster.

I achieved success straight away in my new role based in Austin, Texas. Between my work and Austin's reputation as a fast-growing technology market, my region was chosen to test online subscriptions.

And yes, in today's terms, that would be the early Netflix model. While the history books do not reflect it, Blockbuster was testing online rentals when Netflix entered the industry. In fact, we were also testing with an advantage- movies that could be rented and returned in the store or rented and returned by mail. At that time, Netflix was starting a model based on a distribution center in San Francisco. Initially, that model would be limited to renting online and getting a delivery from the warehouse or distribution center, which usually took two to three days.

After about three months of testing the model, I got a call from one of the leaders in Dallas, the location of our Blockbuster headquarters. The leader indicated that Nigel Travis was going to fly into Austin so that he could see the online subscription model in action. This was a big moment in my career- an opportunity to interact with the president of the company and show off the work that I was doing.

I remember the day vividly. It was Tuesday morning, September 14th, 1999. I waited for Nigel at the Austin airport. This was so long ago that the Austin airport was still in the middle of town and known as Robert Mueller Airport. It was also so far back in time that I could have walked into the terminal and to the gate to meet Nigel. I did not, but I could have. This was before we experienced 9-11.

While I had never met Nigel before, I had done my due diligence-I had pictures of him. As I waited curbside, a rather tall and thin gentleman exited the airport with the look of searching for someone. I suppose that even without a picture, there was no way I could have missed Nigel. Just a description alone made Nigel stand out from the crowd.

I suspected someone had tipped Nigel off as to what I looked like. As I waved him over, it was apparent that he knew I was looking for him.

As Nigel got into the car, I found it odd that no one was traveling with him. It only heightened the anxiety, knowing that I now had the primary responsibility of conversing with Nigel for the entire trip while still focusing on driving. As Nigel began speaking, three things became evident very quickly- one, he was traveling alone because this was the only opportunity on his schedule to see the test in action. Nigel had just arrived on a flight from Tokyo looking at our Blockbuster business there while the rest of the team flew back to the headquarters. I must admit, I was impressed that little Austin, Texas, and this newly promoted regional director, which would be me, had Nigel's full attention after a critical business meeting in Tokyo only hours earlier. The second key learning from the outset was Nigel's fascination for all information- his curiosity was high about all subjects. Third and finally, I was unprepared for his thick British accent that would challenge me throughout the day to translate some of his English dialogue into American colloquialism.

I thought to myself, Nigel had to be jet lagged from the flight's length and the time change. However, you would never know it based on his demeanor- an intense focus on what was in front of him at that moment.

Nigel quickly got past the small talk and got to the online subscription test. As we were in route to the first store, Nigel asked a simple question- how is the online subscription model test going?

Of course, I had spent the previous days rehearsing every potential question Nigel could ask and every possible answer. I would leave no stone unturned. I even used another leader to practice a Q&A session. However, just like a football kicker who can hit field goals from sixty yards in pregame when there is no crowd around and then shank a twenty-yard field goal when it matters in the game with a crowd full of screaming people, my rehearsal experience was no match for the real thing.

Again, this seemed like a simple question to which I thought I had given a simple answer. I quickly responded to Nigel's question with conviction... the test was not going well. There are several issues that we need to address... As I tried to remember the specific details of that day, I ended my sentence there. I stopped because of the dialing that Nigel had initiated. Yes, before I completed the sentence, Nigel was making a phone call. At first, I thought it was rude until I realized the call was directly related to my remarks about the online test.

My response to the question struck a nerve and prompted Nigel to call the Chief Information Officer and respond with the following: "This is Nigel, I am in Austin, Texas, with Joe Thornton, the regional director of operations, and Joe says that there are IT issues with the online subscription model test that have not been resolved and they are keeping us from having success. What are you going to do about it?"

I was speechless. I needed somewhere to hide, which was impossible since I was operating a moving vehicle. I had no expectation that the president of the company would name-drop my name to one of the other executives at that moment. I might as well have been in a mob trial and been called out as a snitch. Yes, I know that sounds melodramatic, but it felt a little bit like that.

I really did not want to be a material witness when it came time to assess the program. Nonetheless, here I was, right in the mix.

To add more anxiety to the situation, I could not hear what the CIO was saying on the other end of the phone. I suppose it was not that material since Nigel did most of the talking, and the responses that he was receiving seemed to be relatively short. It was good that Nigel was not paying attention to my driving, as I am sure I ran a red light or two on the way to the store.

At this point, I did not want Nigel to get off the phone, which meant I would have to deal with the aftermath of that call. But then an interesting thing happened. Nigel hung up the phone, and his tone, while very terse with the CIO, changed immediately.

Nigel thanked me for the feedback and immediately shifted

to talking about the people in the store and whether they felt supported throughout the subscription model test.

As we entered the store, Nigel spent time getting to know the team, and when he began to ask questions about the online subscription model test, it was the most insightful set of questions I could recall at any point in my time as a leader. I have heard it said that you must know the right questions to ask, and on this day, Nigel asked every question of relevance. Nigel understood the big picture, and Nigel understood the small picture. The questions he asked of the store manager and her team were deeply aligned with understanding the day-to-day employee and customer experience and the desire to capture the key learnings of what we could do differently.

The good news is that the attention to detail shifted how the test looked from that day forward. We still had many IT issues, but our overall strategy changed due to the visit. Unfortunately, our technology could not keep pace with our aspirations. But, again, this was very early in the development stage of a subscription model.

Ironically, I found myself working in the headquarters only two short years later, and we were still in the lab trying to figure this out. Ultimately, it was a complete disaster; Netflix overran us, and, as they say, the rest is history.

In reflection, it was clear that if everyone involved in the online subscription model development had the level of attention to detail that Nigel Travis had, we would have had a fighting chance to make it successful; Notwithstanding, we told Reed Hastings, the founder of Netflix, to take a hike when he came calling a year later in Dallas asking us to buy Netflix for $50 million. For Blockbuster, not our finest moment for sure, so we got what we deserved.

Back to Nigel. Nigel was also very astute regarding details when we were in meetings together. Nigel never professed to be the smartest person in the room on any given topic- I would learn later that is a core attribute of a CEO. However, Nigel always had insight on a topic no one else ever seemed to have.

With all this, I believe Nigel's finest moment at Blockbuster was dealing with franchise owners. Again, I am being intentional with my word choice here- 'dealing' with franchise owners.

Many of the franchise owners were, well, a pain in the behind. No, I mean that respectfully. Being there throughout most of the development years of the model, I understood why franchise owners were a pain in the behind. Blockbuster was different than any other business model. Because product went out and came back in, the turn of product generated gross margins unlike anything anyone had ever seen. Franchise owners were accustomed to throwing off unit-level cash historically reserved for businesses five to seven times their size and volume; the profit levels were just that ridiculously good. So good, with any sign of erosion, it drew the ire of the franchise owners... even though many would privately say that they had never earned this type of money in any other business model they had owned.

When negotiating new contracts with our franchise owners, Nigel was always accommodating, coming from what was perceived as "the other side." Nigel would always advocate for the owner's plight, understanding how difficult it is to manage a franchise within a corporate structure- Blockbuster was 85% corporate stores and 15% franchise stores. No detail on the UFOC- Uniform Franchise Offering Circular, now known as the FDD- Franchise Disclosure Document, was too small for Nigel to address. He created a level of trust that I had not seen in a franchise model before.

Of course, when we introduced the end of late fees, all bets were off; all good feelings were gone, and franchise owners lost a significant amount of revenue from late fees that were not nearly offset by customers returning to the brand.

Ironically, as I was penning this chapter, I recently received a call from Nigel. We realized that we had not spoken voice to voice in more than fifteen years, and yes, we picked up right where we left off with recounting stories from the past. Yet another example of Nigel's attention to detail. We would have dinner a few months later, and our reconnection confirmed everything I remembered about his leadership style and attention to detail.

Let me share the story about a second leader who was just as maniacal about attention to detail.

Cliff Burrows. Cliff was an exceptional leader during my time with Starbucks. Cliff is one of the most caring human beings I have ever met. Because he cared so profoundly, he pursued everything with the same passion.

So, I must start this story by sharing how I met Cliff. I had just been promoted to a vice-president role in March of 2008. Around that time, Howard Schultz returned as CEO at Starbucks after an eight-year hiatus from the company.

As you may remember, in 2008, the shakeup in American business had begun... and Starbucks would be no exception. With the financial crisis, Cliff arriving as the new president of US retail, and the return of the former CEO, it meant wholesale changes were coming at Starbucks, mainly because we had no choice but to change.

One of those changes was a decision to close stores. Close stores? What? We did not even know how to do that at Starbucks. I mean, all that we did was open stores- a lot of them and often.

We had to do something to signal that changes were happening to fit the moment of change happening around us and to get ahead of the potential financial ramifications of the recession.

We painstakingly identified approximately six hundred stores across the country for closure. In my geography alone, we had seventy-five locations scheduled to close. Not surprisingly, there was a visceral reaction to the list from field operators across the country. It was a big deal to even consider store closures. Those who supported the idea of closing stores were good as long as it was not "their" stores. Nonetheless, here we were.

I did not scoff at the number of closures or even the disproportionate number of closures within my region. No, not because I knew anything that others did not. Instead, I had just come from Blockbuster only two years earlier. I still had the fresh wounds of a business in turmoil and one that could have at least slowed down the rapid descent by rationalizing the portfolio and closing some of our low-performing locations.

When the Starbucks announcement to close stores was made broadly, the media reacted to it. In this case, I do not blame them- this was different Starbucks news, for sure.

I was at the airport in Dallas, Texas preparing to fly. As I was about to board the plane, my phone rang. This close to boarding, I rarely answer the phone if it is someone I know who cannot get to the point in the limited time available.

I decided to answer this call- one, because it was a 206 area code number- translation, someone calling from Seattle, likely from Starbucks.

Also, under that intense business climate, answering all calls was a wise career move.

I answered. The voice on the other end of the phone said, "Hi, this is Cliff Burrows," or at least that is what I thought he said. Cliff spoke with a very heavy Welsh accent. I do not know that I had ever spoken to anyone from that region of the world. Ironically, Nigel Travis, being from the UK, would be the closest to that. With Cliff, though, it was a combination of being born in one location of the world and spending his time moving around to different countries, so his accent had evolved. Nonetheless, I hung on to every word Cliff said, attempting to decipher his message. Honestly, I missed most of what he said. However, I did catch the key words that helped me understand the purpose of his call.

During this process of store closures, I am not sure that organizationally we had prepared ourselves for the backlash that would ensue. For sure, not in the context of how many stores we were closing. The bottom line was that we were closing "someone's store." Our customers' affinity to a specific Starbucks location was a brand advantage. The impact on "their store" was never more present and evident than at the point of the closure announcement.

To go further, many of the locations slated to close were stores that had only recently been opened, complete with ribbon-cutting ceremonies. Many of these locations were in small-town America. There could not be a worse combination of factors that were in play on the path to shuttering stores.

The move to close was not well-received; it prompted a barrage of calls from angry customers in my geography- most notably, Oklahoma. As I have shared with many people over the years, when you had a Blockbuster Video built in your neighborhood in the 1990s, it put your town on the map; similarly, when you had a Starbucks Coffee location built in your neighborhood in the 2000s, that also put your town on the map and arguably, in an even more relevant way. Well, for sure, at that time because Blockbuster had already run its life cycle.

So, back to the call from Cliff. He had been inundated with emails, calls, and letters from small-town Oklahoma about their Starbucks closing. Even some of the mayors got involved.

Again, while it was challenging to understand every word that Cliff was saying, I did pick up on his tone... and it was intense. Cliff was annoyed, so he got right to it after introducing himself. He wanted to understand why we could not resolve the issue with the locals who took exception to us closing "their" Starbucks location.

My response, with all due respect, was not like we were closing the local hardware store. Starbucks had forged an emotional connection with customers and with the communities themselves. Closing any store was a big deal. There was another crucial factor, though. If we closed a store in Houston, even for a store that was truly a neighborhood location, there were likely other Starbucks locations for the displaced customer within a couple of miles or a couple of blocks, or sometimes even across the street. My list of store closures, though, was about as remote as remote gets.

One of my takeaways from that first encounter with Cliff was that this is personal. Every detail mattered. I am confident that Cliff took the time to read every letter and every email and responded to every phone call made to the office from disgruntled customers. Attention to detail.

Here is another experience during my time working with Cliff: One of my market visits to Dallas with Cliff would occur the following year. It was a visit specifically focused on better understanding the drive-thru lane and how best to evolve the business model as the demand for drive-thru continued to grow.

To get to the root cause, Cliff wanted to visit a few stores of our best performers- great. Cliff wanted to visit in the middle of July- not great.

Typically, when scheduling a market visit months in advance, it is hard to know specific dynamics, like the weather. However, it was July in Texas- I already knew what the weather was going to be like. So, of course, when the day finally arrived for the market visit in Dallas, it was not just summer; it was one of the hottest summer days on record.

And as timing would have it, the visit was between 1:00 pm and 5:00 pm, the peak of Texas heat. What was most memorable about the visit that day was not the conversation; it was the fact that Cliff wanted to stand outside to observe the drive-thru window. So, there we were, outside in suits in 110-degree weather. I tried to focus on the conversation but could not due to my excessive sweating. The interesting thing about Cliff was that he did not have a bead of sweat as we stood outside. Cliff was maniacal about watching cars, customer behavior, and listening intently to what was being ordered at the drive-thru speaker. I learned a lot that day. Some years later, I would ask him about that visit and, of course, he remembered that day. Cliff said that he had spent time in the middle east in the summer, particularly in Kuwait, and the temperature would reach 130 degrees, so the Texas heat did not affect him. At that point, I felt like a sniveling little weenie for complaining about it.

Cliff had a passion for merchandising. So, when he walked into a store on a market visit, he just could not help himself. Cliff specifically had a fascination with water baskets. Oh, the water baskets. Anyone that worked at Starbucks during the Cliff era is undoubtedly reading this and smiling. How can you not? Cliff drove us all crazy with the water baskets. That said, there was always a lesson to learn from his approach. Cliff believed that positioning a tall basket of bottled water right between the point-of-sale registers, literally in the way of the customer, would drive incremental sales. Honestly, I do not know if we ever proved that it drove incremental sales, but I do not believe anyone ever took the time to disprove the effectiveness either, so we were at the mercy of Cliff's idiosyncrasy related to water. Attention to detail.

On another occasion, we visited a store in Stonebriar Mall in Frisco, Texas. In addition to Cliff's approach to this visit, this day was also memorable because I happened to live just down the street from this mall. There was a contingent from Seattle, led by Cliff, and a group of local and regional leaders from my team assembled. We were standing outside the store in the open space of the mall, watching Cliff assess the store. After a few moments, Cliff asked the store design and development leader, who had also flown from Seattle, "Do you see anything wrong with this store?" There was an awkward silence. To reset the conversation, Cliff asked the store design and development leader again what was wrong with the store's aesthetics. Again, an awkward silence. If it felt uncomfortable for me and others on the visit, I suspect the design and development leader wanted to hide under a rock... except that we were inside a mall with no rocks.

The best way to describe the moment is in the movie "Goodfellas," when the gang sits around a table, and Joe Pesci's character asks Ray Liotta's character what was so funny. It will help you to understand the context of this story if you have seen the movie. I am sure that Ray Liotta's character soiled his pants during this scene... and I am most certain that the design and development leader did too, during this store visit. By the way, the "issue" that Cliff detected was that the channel letter Starbucks sign above the door was slightly tilted, and I do mean slightly. I suspect that if we stood there long enough, we could all see it, but not without using a leveler. Attention to detail.

I used to believe that Cliff did this intentionally, but he was just that way- every detail mattered.

And then there was the bone-dry cappuccino. Again, any Starbucks alums will laugh at this one for sure.

Cliff's go-to drink was a bone-dry cappuccino. Cliff enjoyed coaching and teaching baristas how to make it. It is basically an espresso shot and air- it is really bone dry- with just a hint of foam. The cup feels empty when you get it right. Now, some baristas got it right, and, to Cliff's credit, he would tell them how well they did.

For those that did not get his bone-dry cappuccino exactly right, Cliff would often wait and watch as they remade it. Basically, the maximum amount of pressure possible.

In the end, the lessons learned were significant. There are many examples that I am sure that I have forgotten, but I have not forgotten the focus, no matter what the topic.

Nigel and Cliff provided many life and leadership lessons that I still carry with me to this day. Attention to detail matters.

Paying attention to detail behavior demonstrates to people that you care; it is also a demonstration that everything matters- there is no room for indifference. Paying attention to detail is also an example of going the extra mile.

CHAPTER *9:*

Going The Extra Mile

Going the extra mile- I know, so cliché. What does it really mean? What does it get you?

First, going the extra mile is relevant to the topic of mediocrity. Going the extra mile moves you closer to greatness than almost anything else you can do. Of course, extra never guarantees success, but your odds shoot way up, and, sometimes just as important, others recognize that effort. In a work setting, that is usually your peers, your boss, or your boss's boss, so it does matter.

In personal matters, going the extra mile can build trust. You become known as someone who is dependable, consistent, and demonstrates a deep commitment for all that you do. I know, not always the sexy adjectives, but in times of need, the attribute of going the extra mile rises to the top of importance.

Going the extra mile is an idiom, a figurative meaning that is not easily deduced from its literal meaning. Like "It's raining cats and dogs" means that it is raining hard, but the phrase does not accurately indicate that this is what it means. Another is someone "seeing the light." This means someone finally realizes something. There is no light. Native speakers use idioms all the time, most subconsciously. Tying the points together here, "Going The Extra Mile" has nothing to do with running, walking, or distance.

Going the extra mile means going above and beyond what is expected, making a more significant effort than is required, or exerting special energy to accomplish something. To say that someone will go the extra mile is a compliment, acknowledging when someone puts forth more effort than others or than is expected. Those who exert this type of effort often find themselves on the right side of success and constantly stave off mediocrity in the process.

Years ago, I was having dinner with a former colleague, Fred, and the topic of marriage came up. Fred and his wife were about to celebrate their third wedding anniversary. After congratulating him, Fred turned to me and asked, "How have you been able to make your marriage last so long?"

At that time, my wife and I had just celebrated our twentieth wedding anniversary. Of course, Fred and I had the obligatory conversation about the seven-year-itch. I did not say much about it as I believed it could be different for everyone, and I did not want to taint his view of what could come when they reached that mark.

However, we went much deeper in this conversation than I would typically go because I could see that this conversation piqued his curiosity. So, I went in.

My first comment in response to the question from my eager listener was this:

I often hear comments from those having issues with their marriage that become telltale factors. The most often uttered statement is:

"I have done my part in the marriage, so why is my marriage not working?"

I mean, the answer seems so simple. You need not be a marriage counselor to figure this out. However, if you have never been married or are newly married, the answer may not be so obvious.

My comment to Fred as to how I addressed this question was, "You have to be willing to go more than fifty percent, go more than fifty percent more often than you would like, and, to the point of this chapter, be prepared to go the extra mile at any moment for anything." I could tell from Fred's facial reaction that this sounded like a heavy answer he was unprepared to hear. In fact, it is a very heavy answer because marriage is a serious commitment. It requires a level of emotional involvement that differs from any other type of relationship.

I could also tell that Fred did not completely understand the answer either. So, I gave Fred examples, like, in my marriage, when one of our jobs demanded more time than usual. A situation like that required the other one to step up and spend more time with the kids or cleaning the house. Doing more than your fifty percent also shows up when one person in the marriage is sick. The "for richer or for poorer, in sickness and health, until death do us part" stuff is real.

So, what is going the extra mile, then?

Well, I will answer it this way:

It is unique to the individual and the situation. Depending on what is needed to remedy this situation will determine how you define going the extra mile. I know this answer sounds very vague. It is intentionally ambiguous.

Many of our life situations cannot be resolved with a canned answer.

However, let me provide a specific example.

I have seen many couples, most relatively new in their marriage or relationship, struggle with becoming parents. Now, to be fair, parenting is one of the most difficult things many of us will do in our lives, and there truly is no manual for it. However, this is where the "fifty percent" rule comes into play. I have seen couples literally and figuratively hand off the baby once their fifty percent of the time was complete. This usually comes with a verbal command such as, "It is your time to change the baby, it is your time to feed the baby, or it is your turn to get up with the baby."

Seriously, the sheer effort of attempting to make anything 50-50 is difficult enough, like taking a beverage from a bottle and pouring it equally into two cups... and that is on something simple, quantitative, and finite.

Anyone that has raised a child knows that words like unpredictable and unexpected are more representative of the parenting experience. Nonetheless, there are times when I have seen parents stand righteously in their corner after completing their half of the action.

To that, I say, good luck with that approach.

The real question, and I mean a serious question, is this: when you have done your fifty percent, and the other person can only fulfill forty percent, what happens to the other ten percent? Well, there is a gap.

I am not an expert on relationships, nor am I a mathematician. Actually, I am really good at math, but I digress. The point here is obvious:

The gap must be filled; if no one is willing to step up and fill it, terrible things usually happen in the relationship. And for this part, I am speaking from experience.

Also, the solution is relatively simple- the person at fifty percent needs to step forward and fill the gap for the other person who cannot fulfill their fifty percent for whatever reason. Yes, this is a simple solution, but difficult to accept when you are the one who is "right."

It is likely, probably more of a certainty, that if you stay in a marriage long enough, there will be a time when you are on the short side of the stick on effort due to life circumstances and will need your partner to do more than their fifty percent. That is just how life works. I am not a marriage counselor and will never be mistaken for one. However, anyone who has 'skinned their knees' during their marriage and cares an ounce about your marriage and bears witness to their own marital challenges to you, please listen to them.

So, do not "hand the baby off to each other." Go the extra mile for your life partner. I believe you will be glad that you did.

I know I am spending a lot of time on this notion of fifty percent. It is essential because it is a milestone you must pass before going the extra mile. It is mathematically logical- the extra mile is somewhere beyond doing your part.

By the way, with my friend Fred, I will go out on a limb and say that the wisdom I shared with him did not stick; he was divorced only a year later.

Metaphorically speaking, going the extra mile is also about resetting the finish line. Human tendency is to "pull up" as we get close to the proverbial finish line. However, when you can mentally reset before getting to the previously defined finish line, it helps you maintain your current momentum. I know this seems logical.

Except to say, there are plenty of videos on the internet showing runners, cyclists, or ice skaters who were so close to victory and decided to cruise through the finish line only to be clipped at the end by someone else who was finishing with much more purpose and aggression. I have seen those videos, and I can only shake my head. After all the arduous work that has been put in, day after day, month after month, and in some situations like the Olympics, year after year, it does not make sense to give it all up on a lack of effort at the very end. But it happens.

So, what does going the extra mile look like in a business setting? Well, it is certainly doing more than your fifty percent. In part because there is not always a partner in your work relationship, per se. Actually, there are times when having multiple partners makes it difficult to assign responsibility, at least evenly assign it. It also makes the finish line more challenging to identify and the effort needed for success much more difficult to quantify. However, that is not all bad. Here is why:

There have been many starts to a fiscal year in businesses where I have worked when we did not have our budget prepared when the year began. On the one hand, that was problematic because no one knew what their target was to achieve financial success. On the other hand, I like to live in this process because the sky is the limit. If you do not have a target to aim for, I have always said to aim high. There is a potential risk of having a target, which is your focus on the target. If the target is too low, well, you can see where I am going with this.

This is why going the extra mile is not necessarily quantitative. This is a crucial distinction in this discussion. Attempting to quantify what the extra mile looks like can be a throttle on the possibility of success... and land you in the 50-40-10% relationship gap threshold I described earlier.

So, what do the benefits of going the extra mile look like? First, it will bring you more opportunities. Sometimes, tremendous opportunities.

Take, for example, this story:

Many years ago, an elderly lady was strolling through a Pittsburgh Department Store, killing time. She passed counter after counter without anyone paying any attention to her. All the clerks had spotted her as a "looker" who had no intention of buying. They even made it a point of looking in another direction when she stopped at their counters.

Finally, the lady came to a counter attended by a young clerk who politely asked if he might serve her. "No," she replied. "I am just biding my time, waiting for the rain to stop so I can go home."

"Very well, madam," the young man said with a smile. "May I bring out a chair for you?" He brought it without waiting for her answer.

After the rain slacked, the young man took the old lady by the arm, escorted her to the street, and bade her goodbye. As she left, she asked him for his card.

Several months later, the store's owner received a letter asking that this young man be sent to Scotland to take an order for the furnishings of a home.

The store owner wrote back that he was sorry, the young man did not work in the house furnishings department. But he explained that he would gladly send an "experienced man" to do the job.

Back came a reply that no one would do except this particular young man. The letter was signed by Andrew Carnegie who, at one point, would become the wealthiest man in the world, and the "house" he wanted to be furnished was Skibo Castle in Scotland.

The elderly lady that had been in the department store shopping months earlier was Carnegie's mother. The young man was sent to Scotland.

He received an order for several thousand dollars' worth of household furnishings and a partnership in the store. He later became the owner of a half interest in the store.

Pretty cool. That is what going the extra mile got this young man.

Sometimes the extra mile can be found in the little additions. The stuff you throw in... or, as in the case of this young man, good old-fashioned kindness.

So, what do some other elements of going the extra mile in a business setting look like?

First, taking responsibility for something that was not your fault can still be your responsibility. While it would be easy to blame someone else when your customers are dissatisfied, it is not a good look and will not benefit your brand in the long term. Literally, the last thing the customer wants to hear is that you cannot resolve their issue, or you are not responsible for their problem. Either one will garner a negative response from your customer and ultimately erode any brand loyalty that has been built. I have seen leaders take responsibility for service-related issues that were presented as a customer's problem, only to investigate and determine that the fault was, in fact, internally. Interesting how that works. So, swallow your pride, take the lumps, and live to fight another day to build your brand.

Second, never forget that humans want to feel valued. They want to feel like everything they say is heard and understood; you are the trusted provider to make that happen. Even if the customer's mind is elsewhere, knowing that yours is on them will matter.

A former restaurant owner remembers when a regular customer dined without his wife. "Knowing that he normally came with her, we asked if she was okay, and he let us know she was sick and bedridden. Before the customer left, we packed up some freshly made bread, soups, and other menu items for him to take home to her, on the house. The customer was overwhelmed by our kind gesture, but I had been just as overwhelmed by his loyalty over the years."

This level of connection and care will create brand loyalty for a lifetime.

Third, take control when things are not right and make them right. Companies that measure loyalty and provide tools to service-related organizations often wax poetically about the power of service recovery. In fact, there are many testimonials that more brand loyalty is built from recovery than from day-to-day service.

Fourth, seek feedback. Customers, clients, and workers will gladly give you feedback, but often you must ask for it. This can be true of personal relationships as well. It is like asking your teenage son how his day at school went. Expect the one-word answer- good. The point is that if you want to know more, you must probe and ask the right questions.

While it might seem a bit unorthodox in a relationship, imagine the power of you asking your spouse or significant other for feedback or ways to improve. I promise you that conversation will breed something positive. In addition, you will be given credit for your effort.

I guess you should also be prepared for the "Did I do something wrong? and "Why are you being so nice?" questions.

Deliver exceptionally on the simple things, give a little extra, take responsibility and control, personalize the experience, and remember what they forget. Push toward the extra mile and exceed the expectations of your clients.

Going the extra mile is muscle that you must flex often so that it becomes a part of everything you do. There is a subtle but powerful mental attitude connected with it.

Let me share one last story inside this chapter that has to do with going the extra mile:

With the heavy amount of air travel that I have done for the better part of thirty years, I had often whisked by local shoeshine shops in the airports wondering, what is the big deal- my shoes look fine just as they are. As my dress shoes got a bit fancier over the years, I began to pay more attention to the shoeshine exchange occurring in every airport of scale- not the process of cleaning the shoes, but the interaction between patron and service provider.

Then one day, it was time for me to try this shoeshine thing.

Sitting in the chair, I immediately began to get it. In reflection, there is no other way that I would have understood it without sitting in the chair. I quickly became fixated on the meticulous nature of the process. Because of the level of detail, there were a few occasions during the process where I thought the shoeshine person was done, but then he would add one more step. There was a bit of stress as I had a plane to catch, and I had no idea this process would take more than twenty minutes. But with every deliberate stroke, my shoes came to life even more, and I thought less about watching the clock. Undoubtedly, it was worth the time, the money, and especially the conversation.

I also realized that during a hectic day, and arguably in the most hectic environment, being in the airport, it felt a little like there was a bubble around my experience. The airport did not sound quite as loud; I was not in quite as much of a rush because of the engaging conversation, and I suppose any activity that slows your heart rate and gets your blood pressure down in an airport is a good thing.

I was not treated any differently than anyone else who sat in that seat, but it certainly felt like this shoeshine provider was going the extra mile just for me. So much so that I was shocked when he concluded and said that all I owed him was ten dollars. I handed him a twenty-dollar bill and bade him farewell. I wanted desperately to tell him that he was undercharging, but I also did not want to be the one to give him advice that prices him right out of business.

Ultimately, going the extra mile is an intentional act, driven by demonstrating effort. However, you should be careful. Every part of our life runs the risk of being met with cynicism. Giving extra effort is not immune to this either. If you always go the extra mile, you could be labeled as an overachiever.

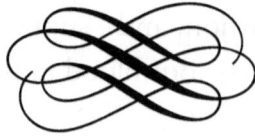

CHAPTER 10:

The Overachievers

Overachievers sometimes get a bad rap. Let me correct that, overachievers almost always get a bad rap. That is why the term exists. However:

Overachievers are often called overachievers only by underachievers.

Underachievers do not always do it due to being envious or jealous; however, I would be careful not to underestimate the nefarious intentions of either of those emotions. Seeing someone else achieve something you have not achieved does not always feel good- even if the emotion is directed toward what you did not do versus what the other person accomplished. Nevertheless, calling someone an overachiever does not often show up well. I get it; often, it is said in jest. That said, almost every joke has a message someone attempts to convey without saying it directly.

Underachievers are potentially keeping those would-be overachievers from achieving the things for which they are striving. I know, it probably feels like a sermon is coming. That is because there is a sermon coming:

Underachievers is the title of the sermon. Look, we cannot all be great all the time, but we certainly should not surround ourselves with those who are not suitable for us any of the time. Can I get an amen?

Seriously, this is a problem. A big problem. Keeping an underperformer on your team at work is one thing, but keeping a substandard performer in your personal space is a real problem... or both.

I am not done preaching.

Keeping underachievers around in your personal life is concerning because it may... okay, I am being too kind, it will hinder achieving all that you aspire to achieve. However, I believe there are times when we keep the low performer around in our personal life to boost our own self-esteem. Just like the person that keeps the less-than-attractive friend around so that they are the best pick of the two when going to the bar or anywhere else to be seen. I know, I went there.

The point of making yourself feel good at the expense of someone else is a character check, but I will not judge anyone on that. Instead, I am going to go to the productivity aspect of it. Your performance is likely suffering because you are "playing down to the competition"- you are not working hard enough to improve yourself... because you do not have to.

As a mother or father, playing one-on-one in basketball against your fifteen-year-old son will be competitive and may lead you to the defeat you knew was coming someday. Playing against your seven-year-old son, probably not so much. If you have any ability at all, there is a good chance that you will win easily over your second grader. The bottom line is that your seven-year-old will get better from playing against better competition- you. However, not only will you not get better, but you may see your skills erode. Same concept here- it may be fun to know that you will come out on top playing against your seven-year-old son, but it is just another form of boosting your self-esteem... at the expense of your own child. I know, right? When I put it in those terms, it feels a little self-serving.

I am doing you a favor by saying this. I know it does not feel good, but you are headed straight for mediocrity unless you change the equation and become the less attractive friend in the pair. Sometimes growth hurts, and I am being serious in this chapter about avoiding underachievers. I will be repetitive here: I do not write self-help books; I write self-reflection books. If I give it to you easy, nothing will change.

I will not charge you for this sermon- it is on me. Well, you did buy my book, and I am not an ordained minister, so I will call it even.

As discussed earlier in the book, many risks come from comparing yourself to someone else. What I am describing here is even more damaging.

Of course, all of this applies to the business setting as well. However, if I had started with business first, you would not have heard me.

In business, we sometimes find comfort with those who are underperforming, especially those in the same workgroup. Do not do that. It is condescending, and again, you are stunting your own development. Now, you may not be saying condescending things to the lower performer, but trust me, your demeanor is... no matter how subtle it may be.

So, how do you take this information, move towards greatness, and move away from mediocrity? Let me walk through a few thoughts for your consideration:

Start by loving what you do. Pursuing anything you are not passionate about is simply a waste of time. I get it; some people are positioned by their parents or family lineage to become a doctor or an attorney, attend a specific college, or enter the military. Oh wait, I feel someone in denial as they are reading this passage. Let me digress for a moment here:

Planting ideology is a real thing, it happens often, and it is damaging to your children. Parents, if your child follows in your footsteps, please make sure it was their choice and not one you manufactured for them before they had a collective memory, thought, or the courage to say no. Many parents with small children may be shaking their heads and saying, "He is not talking about me." Actually, I am. Every flag you hoist, every television and radio station, every bumper sticker, every political vote, and every church. You are influencing all of that in your child.

I hope people reading this book go "against the grain" and make their own decisions. If it is not something you are personally passionate about, even at an early age, you are going to regret it, on some level, later in life. You may praise your parents if the brainwashing leads to success, but you will also curse them simultaneously.

For any readers, if there is a burden your parents have placed on you about religion, the military, politics, or a school choice, please have this conversation with them. Intentionally, I did not reference only young readers. There are 50-year-old adults still living scared under the ideology of their elderly parents.

I am intentionally digressing and being repetitive here. What you are teaching your child may not be to see the world as it is, but as you see it. These two things are not the same.

I suspect many overachievers will read this and disagree with me and may go as far as saying their maniacal push to drive their kids led to their kid's success. To those parents, I highly recommend asking your children if you have influenced their decisions and if they are happy with the outcome. Do it with some decorum, tact, and humility, or do not waste your time. Asking leading-the-witness type questions will get you the answer you want but potentially have your child questioning your motive for even asking.

Back to the topic at hand- if it is your hand-selected passion that you are following, that is outstanding.

Loving what you do means that you will be willing to put in the time to pursue it, thus dramatically increasing your chances of success... and happiness. I have only lived one life I know of, but I have been fortunate to live vicariously through the lives of hundreds of other successful people, and I have listened very carefully to their laments. Listening to the success stories is the easy part; hearing them talk about their regrets and grudges is much more interesting... and painful. However, I can do something with that- share cautionary tales with others. That is why I am including these experiences in this book.

Well, there is a lot to digest here already. How do you break free from this? Who or what, then, are you supposed to leave behind?

Start with leaving the problem people behind.

Also, leave the unsolvable problems behind.

In the end, overachieving is simply doing more than expected. Not sure how that can be considered a bad thing.

You must be careful here, though. Being called an overachiever can also be an inference that no one expected you to be successful or to be this successful, though it could be the very thing that inspired you to work so hard to achieve. Very tricky. Let me give you an example:

You can take any craft to illustrate an overachiever, but if you follow my writings, you know I like to use sports as an analogy. Mostly because sports are relatable, and there are tangible results that can amplify the story.

This is a good moment to discuss Tony Romo, the former quarterback of "America's Team," the Dallas Cowboys.

Romo is often criticized for racking up a bunch of statistics while playing for Dallas but never guiding them to the Super Bowl. At the printing of this book, Romo holds almost all the Cowboys team passing records, including passing touchdowns, passing yards, most games with at least three hundred passing yards, and games with three or more touchdown passes. Dak Prescott will likely pass Romo on all these lists someday soon. However, Romo's reputation was affected by a lack of postseason success, having won only two of the six playoff games he appeared in and never advancing beyond the divisional round. His 97.1 passer rating is the highest in National Football League History among retired quarterbacks who never appeared in the Super Bowl.

I have asked my friends, who are lifelong Dallas Cowboys fans, if they had to pick one quarterback from the history of the Cowboys franchise to start a team, who would it be? Troy Aikman, Roger Staubach, or Tony Romo? Of course, almost all of them choose anyone but Romo. In fact, a couple of them threw in a write-in pick of Danny White over Tony Romo. I know, that was harsh.

I believe that it is all fair criticism, though... hear me out:

After all, this is sports, Romo played the most highly visible position in all of sports, and he did it on the most recognizable sports franchise in the world. So yes, criticism comes with the territory.

I heavily criticized Romo during his playing days for all these reasons, but mostly because he fumbled his way into the national spotlight, literally. In Romo's very first playoff game, he was the holder for the kicker on what would be a game-winning chip-shot field goal. In football reference, his job on this play was as easy as any role on a football field. All Romo had to do was catch the ball, put it down on the ground, and let the kicker win the game. Unfortunately, the ball must have had butter on it because Romo fumbled a perfect snap, which prevented the kicker from kicking it, leaving Romo only one option- pick the ball up and run it into the end zone to win the game. As Romo took off, he was tackled on the one-yard line. Game over. Season over.

I mean, this was some Lucy and Charlie Brown stuff, but at least Charlie Brown got a swing at the ball. Romo basically left the kicker "at the altar," as the kicker never even got the opportunity to kick the ball. Romo getting tackled on the one-yard line is a metaphor for his career. He almost got to the finish line, but in the end, he snatched defeat from the jaws of victory.

To further amplify how unexpected this play was is the fact that quarterbacks rarely took on the role of the holder for field goal kicks- it was almost exclusively the backup quarterback or the punter that was best suited to do so. Needless to say, Romo did not hold for any field goals after that debacle, nor did any other starting NFL quarterbacks- that was the end of that.

If it sounds like I am having fun with Romo's lack of success, I am. He was one of very few quarterbacks during his time of playing that lost games with mishaps or interceptions at the worst moment.

NFL coaches often tell their quarterbacks to "not lose the game," and most of them do not. They become labeled as "game managers." Game manager is not a term of endearment in football, but even that is a level above the reputation that Tony Romo created for himself.

He choked. Fair or not, Romo's career was defined at that moment by fumbling the hold on the game-winning kick.

Romo's inability to get the Cowboys to a Super Bowl, or even to the NFC Championship, over the next decade would further cement his legacy of choking when the team needed him the most.

However, as harsh as all this is, I have a unique perspective on Tony Romo... he is an overachiever. Wait, what? After all that negativity? Yes, let me explain:

- Tony Romo has one of the highest playoff passer ratings in the fourth quarter in NFL history.
- The two playoff wins that Romo had in his NFL career were driven by key, last-second passes by Romo.
- Romo was undrafted out of Eastern Illinois and arguably one of the top ten most successful undrafted players ever.

Okay, this last point is really important. To achieve what Tony Romo achieved makes this argument:

Tony Romo was as good as he was going to get. What we observed was his max performance. I know my Dallas Cowboy friends and readers will vehemently disagree with me on this perspective. With all due respect, Cowboys fans will disagree on anything that puts their team or players in a negative light. Yes, all sports team fans do that, but Dallas Cowboys fans are special... and that is not meant to be a compliment.

I will restate the obvious point I am making here: Tony Romo was an overachiever.

From what the situation and odds suggest, Romo becoming a starting quarterback in the NFL was a big deal. Having any success at all was an even bigger deal; playing for over a decade as a starting quarterback was a really big deal.

Romo was as good as he was going to get... and achieved more than expected against the odds.

By the way, Tony Romo present-day as an NFL color commentator is outstanding. Truly best-in-class. I listen to his play-by-play analysis and Romo often sees things that others do not see before the ball is snapped. So, in the end, I can be fair in my assessment of Tony Romo.

Ultimately, Tony Romo should be celebrated for what he accomplished in his NFL career, not vilified.

Overachievers generally do not leave the results to chance... primarily because of their insatiable desire to succeed. Instead, they take the negative energy from naysayers and go forward with a proverbial 'chip on their shoulder' as their motivation. I suspect Romo had a bit of this in his DNA on his way to the NFL.

The bottom line is that overachievers do not allow themselves to land in the space of mediocrity either... they just don't. If for no other reason, their level of paranoia will not let them go there. Paranoia can then become a vicious cycle. I am not saying this state of being is healthy, but I submit that it is not necessarily unhealthy either.

There are many dimensions to consider when discussing overachievers. I have not mentioned the insecurity overachievers carry on their daily journey. It would seem that overachievers are highly confident people. However, fear and insecurity are often far more prevalent than confidence. There is a constant fear of not being good enough. I will come back to fear shortly.

Insecure overachievers often doubt their worth, especially in highly competitive environments, so they work harder and harder to compensate.

In the work environment, people know they are being measured against their colleagues. However, because they do not know how their colleagues are doing, overachievers set incredibly lofty standards for themselves, just to be sure.

If insecurity exists for too long in the mind of an overachiever, it will need to be addressed, but how?

Well, you can influence how you respond to the insecurity.

First, recognize your triggers. Others around you may intentionally create an environment that causes you to show your insecurities. Awareness of any innate emotional trigger is critical- not just for success in the boardroom but also in your personal life.

Second, define success in your own terms, not others. This is a critical component. Nothing screams insecurity like achieving success only to find that others have moved the finish line on you or perceived to have done so. If you are confident in the goals that you have set, do not allow yourself to second guess your approach later. Also, remember a tenet of being an overachiever is you likely have set a goal that is much more ambitious than those around you. Yet another element that will bring the naysayers out in full force.

And third, respect the evidence of and celebrate your success. This is sometimes the hardest element for an overachiever to grasp. An overachiever will talk a good game about celebrating their success. Meanwhile, they are behind the scenes planning their next project. This is the way the mind of an overachiever works.

But this maniacal drive is not necessarily a bad thing- it is one of the ways overachievers keep score for themselves. They are out to change the world. And, in reality, the best and brightest overachievers are not competing with you. You are literally not worthy of their competition. They see themselves as their most formidable foe.

That said, there is a shadow side to overachievement. As is often said among human resources professionals assessing competencies, a strength overused can become a weakness. This can be true of overachievement as well.

While this overachieving behavior can lead to professional and academic success, it can create a massive imbalance in a person's life. Overachievers may neglect the needs of everyone around them and, ultimately, their own needs.

Achievement is a good thing, but you must always consider the sacrifice you are making. If the achievement jeopardizes your health, happiness, and relationships, you should reconsider whether it is worth it.

Overachievers tend to be remarkably successful in their professional lives but are often known as hard-driving workaholics.

As a result, team members may respect an overachiever's work ethic but can feel overburdened by the weight of these leaders' expectations.

Work is not the only area in which overachievement is common. Striving to be perfect at parenting, housework, and hobbies are just a few other areas where overachievement can occur.

One more perspective on this topic. I believe there are four questions to ask yourself that help assess your level of overachievement behavior.

Are You a Perfectionist? Overachievers may sometimes become overly concerned with being perfect. For an overachiever, not being perfect is a sign of failure.

Just as achievement is usually a good thing, being a perfectionist is not always bad news. It often means you value excellent work and are committed to doing your best. However, when this perfectionism becomes a source of stress and anxiety, it can take a toll on your physical and mental well-being.

Perfection is an elusive goal. In fact, it is an aspiration, not a destination. Well, that is the logic of it all. But do not tell that to an overachiever. They believe perfection is within reach. Overachievers are simply wired differently; therefore, in their minds, the pursuit of perfection is at least a possibility. While the rest of us know better than to chase the notion of perfection, overachievers believe they will discover something the rest of us do not know.

Ever Feel Satisfied? Satisfaction is a feeling that often evades overachievers. An overachiever may declare satisfaction, but it lasts for only a moment. The urge to take on the next conquest is too strong to resist. Resting on their laurels seems unproductive, so the next goal is just over the horizon. If you are feeling this, you fall squarely within the space of being an overachiever.

Overachievers often view the word satisfaction itself as underachievement. The core belief of an overachiever is that there must be something more, something better.

The lack of satisfaction will be evident to those close to the overachiever. This is important to note- if you have people in your inner circle that are constantly telling you that you do not stop to celebrate your successes, then you really should heed their advice.

Do You Feel Stretched Too Thin? In addition to working too hard, overachievers will take on additional work... a lot of additional work. The challenge of doing their own work is often not enough for an overachiever. There is a desire to prove they are the best and can take on the most.

There is a lesson here. Overachievers often believe that saying no is a weakness- quite the contrary. Saying yes to everything shows that you lack the courage to say no when the situation requires you to say no.

Being stretched too thin and not achieving the expected outcome often leaves an overachiever contemplating what could have been. If you are in this headspace, talk to someone about it. You are likely selling yourself short and falling prey to overachievement.

Are You Motivated by Fear? There are many different sources of motivation and, as I mentioned earlier in the chapter, fear happens to be one of them.

I subscribe to the theory that there is good and bad fear. Good fear can motivate and inspire. In the context of an overachiever, it is often good fear that causes you to commit or over-commit. Unfortunately, it does not take much for that good fear to tip over and become bad fear.

When I think about good fear versus bad fear, I can see a few circumstances where we can either experience good fear and act or allow bad fear to rule our lives, severely limiting our options, outcomes, and potential results. Overachievers are often motivated by fear- a bit of a 'bring it on' mentality. Here are a few examples of good fear versus bad fear:

Feeling nervous and afraid before you step on stage to deliver a presentation is okay. That is good fear. It becomes bad fear when you do not get on the stage at all.

It is okay to feel a bit anxious and nervous before a job interview. That is good fear. It is bad fear if you allow it to stop you from applying for jobs and advancing your career.

It is okay to be a little scared on your wedding day. That is good fear. It is bad fear when you do not show up for the wedding and avoid committing to that someone special in your life.

It is okay to pause before sharing your ideas and opinions in a meeting when you know that not everyone will agree. That is good fear. It is bad fear when you feel as though you cannot speak your mind, make valid points, refuse to contribute to a discussion, and say nothing.

Fear is a normal and primal emotion that everyone experiences. Not all fear is bad; after all, being afraid is a mechanism that keeps us alive at times; it is called survival instinct. And it is okay to feel fear when we are doing something that we are not used to doing, doing something for the first time, or when the stakes are high.

Overachievers still experience fear, just like everyone else. However, they can differentiate between good fear and bad fear and do not allow fear to stop them from doing what they believe matters.

In the end, overachievers often understand why they are overachievers and are willing to accept the tradeoffs that come with this label. If you take this posture of an overachiever in your career, future, and relationships, the odds are in your favor to succeed.

No matter the level of success, I believe you will always be rewarded for your effort... especially high-spirited effort.

CHAPTER 11:

Effervescent Effort

I see people striving for excellence in many areas of life, both personally and professionally... which is incredibly inspiring. However, it is not always the result that is so inspirational- sometimes, it is the effort. Effort matters.

Effervescent effort, even more so. Spirited, energetic, lively, enthusiastic- that is effervescent. Effervescent effort is real effort, not the manufactured stuff people talk about just to get their nose above mediocre with their effort. What do I mean? Start with this one:

People often say things like, "I gave it 110%." Of course, you did not- 100% is the maximum.

I know; it is a figure of speech. No matter, it is still not true, and this is an important distinction. Careless terms like this can unintentionally devalue what 100% really means. Think about the number of times in your life when you can say you ran as fast or as long as you could, lifted the most weights you could lift, or practiced playing an instrument until you had calluses on your hands. None of these examples truly represent 100%, as they each possess a level of subjectivity, but as close as you felt you could get to 100%. You can remember what it felt like... the complete exhaustion, which, by the way, could be physical or mental. That is real effort- "maximum effort." I would prefer someone give an accurate number representing their effort, like 84%, versus a reckless term like '110%.'

People who give maximum effort are usually left standing at the end of a long race or achieving academic or career success- it just works that way.

Effort is usually tied to passion. Passion is typically connected to excellence. Excellence will drive out mediocrity.

Effort is not about delivering best-in-class results or achieving everything you set out to do. Effort is a behavior. And yet, incredible effort can dramatically increase your chances of landing those great results- this, too, just works that way.

I have a story of effort that I witnessed recently. I visited Denver, Colorado, to see an old friend and former colleague named Frank. It had been years since we had worked together. As with most relationships that get impacted by a life change- job, family, relationships- the time spent together changes swiftly, and before you know it, years have passed. This was our situation.

When I arrived, we discussed what we would like to do with

our time. We could have stayed in the city, but our time was limited, and every minute would count, so getting away from all distractions seemed to be the thing to do. Frank recommended that we take a ride up Mount Evans. Not knowing the area but trusting Frank, I agreed.

Mount Evans is the highest elevated paved road in North America. We were already a mile high in Denver but decided to go even higher. This was indeed getting off the beaten path.

Frank had thought about our time together and provided further narrative about our adventure. Frank walked me through it in great detail and was eager to share with me the road ahead. This was a spectacular course on the way to the summit of 14,130-foot Mount Evans.

Okay, I will sheepishly admit that we only experienced some of those sites firsthand as we did not hike up to the top of Mount Evans. For starters, we did not have that much time. It would have taken us three days, given our physical disposition, and we were in no mood to try something like this for the first time. Although, I will say, that would have been so much more dramatic for this story. No, instead, we drove up to the top. The view on the way up to 14,130 feet was breathtaking, though... even from the comfortable seat in Frank's truck. It was also a ninety-degree day, so that made our decision easy to enjoy the air-conditioned environment on the way up.

While making our way up, we did make a few stops. Most notably, we stopped at about 9,000 feet at a souvenir shop. As we got out of the truck, we could feel the thinness in the air- a distinct difference from the mile-above-sea-level air we had left only thirty minutes earlier in Denver. Even at that height, getting out of the truck and looking down, way down at Denver, the outline of the city was quite striking... and distant.

At this souvenir shop, we met a gentleman who was biking. We stopped to talk to him and, as we had guessed, he was planning to ride his bike to the top of the mountain. He was dressed in black from head to toe, and although he was a little older than the average cyclist, he seemed to look the part of a serious cyclist, nonetheless.

As we exited the shop, we bid the biker adieu. Then, we continued our trek up to the top, talking and stopping along the way to admire the views and the exotic animals that appeared along the way. Exotic animals? Yes. We saw mountain goats and bighorn sheep grazing along the roadside, lazily staring back at us. We also spotted marmots- giant ground squirrels that live at higher elevations.

As we made our way up the mountain, I kept thinking about the biker. He may have been in great physical shape, but this climb was not for the faint of heart. I was not confident that this trek uphill on a bike was achievable, given the distance, the terrain, and the incredibly thin air. Nonetheless, the biker soon faded from my mind and was replaced with the sensational views of the moment.

It must have taken us about an hour from the souvenir shop

to reach the top. We spent time there taking it all in and, after a short time, began our descent down the mountain. To our surprise, we ran into our biker friend again- he was almost to the top and looking as spry as he did at the souvenir shop many bicycle tire revelations earlier. We were in awe.

We stopped to talk to him. I was listening to what he was saying, but all I could focus on was that he showed no signs of exhaustion and had just as much enthusiasm as he did in the gift shop a couple of hours earlier. True effervescent effort.

The only time I had experienced someone in sweltering temperatures like this without showing any sign of perspiration was visiting Disney World on a business trip many years ago. Of course, Disney is all about effervescent effort too, so... digression alert:

Working at a previous brand, we were opening a new store inside of Disney, and, as a brand, we decided to partner with Disney to do a ribbon-cutting ceremony. This partnership had been in the works for many years, so getting this to the finish line was well worth the planned celebration.

The ribbon-cutting was set for 8:00 am in Orlando, Florida, in July. I lived in Houston, Texas, for years- heavy humidity. I also lived in New Orleans- even heavier humidity, based on the city being well below sea level. But Orlando, this was next-level humidity. Of course, I should have known better...

Only a few short years earlier, my family made a trip to Universal

Studios in Orlando on a balmy July morning as the Harry Potter Experience debuted. The wait in line was for the one shop to open- I certainly wish I had been aware of that before trekking from Texas to Florida.

Yes, most of the Harry Potter setup was just a façade- no, there really were fake storefronts, as they were apparently behind on getting this project completed. This exhibit was officially announced as opening in spring of that year. Technically, they did make their deadline by opening on June 20th, next to the last day of "spring." There was literally one gift shop and the Hogwarts Express, the train. The rest was cardboard, well, not much better material than cardboard.

The wait in line was ultimately worth it- so says my children. The kids caught me at my most vulnerable moment. As we approached the front of the line for entry to the store, my two youngest children asked, "How much can we buy?" I responded, "Buy all the stuff you want because we are not returning and doing this again." I am sure I did not use the word stuff in my response. Nonetheless, I recommended that my children get all the Invisibility Cloaks, wands, and other wizardry things their hearts desired. To their credit, they demonstrated some level of restraint despite my open invitation to go on a shopping spree.

Okay, wow- that was multiple levels of digression. So let me get back to the first digression- the ribbon-cutting ceremony with Disney.

The good news is that I did not have any hair, so I did not have to worry about my hair being ruined by the humidity. However, that meant that any sweat would be clearly visible on my head, and the lack of hair would allow sweat to run down my face more easily- I know, disgusting, but true. And yes, I was sweating like I was taking a lie detector test and knew I was failing.

By contrast, I looked at the representatives from Disney in attendance to represent their brand. Two gentlemen in their mid-thirties appeared with chiseled jaws that would make Gaston from Beauty And The Beast envious and, as you may have guessed, not a bead of perspiration in the sweltering humidity. Even the dancers performing on Main Street wore makeup that somehow defied the odds and stayed intact. Honestly, this was the magic of Disney.

I must give Disney a lot of credit, though. Disney is all about presentation and effort. Being Mickey Mouse is a perfect example of this.

On the outside, looking in, it would seem that being Mickey Mouse is the most desirable job you could have at Disney World or Disneyland. Yes, it would seem... but it is not. On one of my visits to Disney World a few years ago, I had this very conversation with some local Disney leaders. I was shocked to hear this revelation. I had just assumed that everyone wanted to be Mickey Mouse. After all, Mickey Mouse _is_ Disney.

But there are rules to being Mickey Mouse that I never really thought about before:

The costumes are hot and stuffy. There were never any fans in the costume. The costumes are incredibly challenging to get in and out of, so you had better go to the bathroom before you suit up. Also, walk slowly and carefully, and do not swing your arms or legs, as you are basically wearing armor based on the weight of the costume. You could injure a little one passing by.

Do not wear makeup because it will not be on your face by the end of the shift anyway.

You may have to dance too. But do not worry about being embarrassed; your mask will hide your identity.

Ensure no one puts an infant in your arms to take a picture. The gloves are often too thick or loose, making it hard to grip a child.

You must stay in character and never reveal your identity.

You must sign the Mickey Mouse signature a specific way because they want guests to feel as though they are meeting the same Mickey at any Disney Park.

Perhaps the best part of being Mickey Mouse is that you get hugs daily, and people are excited to see you.

All that to say this: The excitement and effervescent effort that Disney applies to all they do is inspiring. Every brand should approach their work in such a way.

I learned a lot about hubris too, at Disney. It is an incredible brand; of course, they make some amazing, timeless movies.

However, even the best studios miss the mark from time to time. Exhibit A- "The Lone Ranger."

The Lone Ranger, starring Johnny Depp, by Hollywood standards, especially considering that it came from Disney, was a colossal flop. One critic described the movie as a "bloated, misshapen mess, a stillborn franchise loaded with metaphors for its feeble attempts to amuse, excite and entertain." And that was one of the kinder reviews. The movie grossed $89 million in U.S. Box Office dollars. By 2013, movies were doing that in the first week, and, considering this movie was released in Hollywood prime time on the Fourth of July weekend, it only further added to the narrative of a box office bomb. If that wasn't bad enough, the movie cost $215 million to make.

If I did not have an extensive background working for Blockbuster and watching thousands of movies over the years, perhaps I would not be able to articulate how significant the box office shortfall really was.

As I was visiting the Disney campus in late September of 2013, the subject of the Lone Ranger movie came up in conversation. Listening to Disney people talking about it, you would have believed that it was the movie of the year. I am being serious. The amount of hubris within the brand did not allow them to consider anything a disaster... even when it was. I really could not believe what I was hearing. When I challenged it, based on my movie knowledge, there was no giving in. Disney was spectacular, and so was everything that they did, and that was that. Almost cult-like... but I mean that in the most endearing way.

So, I know this story sounds like a negative slant on Disney-quite the contrary. The genuine, enthusiastic energy about their brand was something to behold. And it made sense. Disney is not associated with mediocrity in any way. Disney has been maniacal about creating an experience, and they will have nothing to do with coming up short of that. This passion has endured for generations.

I walked away incredibly inspired... and in awe of their effervescent effort. All this after talking about what appeared to be a failure to the rest of civilization. By the way, I still could not bring myself to see the Lone Ranger movie. Life is already too short- I could not waste another two and a half hours on this movie.

Okay. I have strayed to an unhealthy place.

Back to the cyclist. He was incredibly committed to achieving his goal of cycling to the top of Mount Evans. He was effervescent in his approach, and his effort was unwavering.

Let me change gears and talk about a leader who demonstrated effervescent effort.

At thirty years old, I worked for Blockbuster Video and was promoted to my first regional director of operations job. I had a great run leading up to this opportunity and believed I was ready for it. Maybe I was too confident that I was prepared for it. I was the hot commodity in the company at the time, and I went hard charging into that role.

Just as I was settling into my new role, there was a realignment in the structure, and the person who promoted me left the company. I felt vulnerable. I must admit, there was a bit of nervous energy going into a new role, relocating to a new market, and getting a new boss simultaneously. In the process, I would learn that getting a new boss was the most beneficial aspect of the structure change.

The person that I would be working for was a leader named Eileen Terry. I knew nothing about her before her move into the zone vice president role. I quickly learned that she was nothing like the person who promoted me... but that was not a bad thing.

The first time we spoke was during the Martin Luther King Jr. Holiday in 1999, shortly after she took over the role. I had been in the regional director position for about four months. Long enough to get relocated and know where the restroom was in my new office. Other than that, I was pretty green.

I would say that I was a good leader. I demonstrated enough leadership to be noticed and given this promotion without asking for it. However, under Eileen Terry's leadership, I became a much better leader.

I will refer to Eileen as ET for the rest of the story. She preferred to be called ET, but I will admit it was initially weird. Of course, all I could picture was ET from the Steven Spielberg movie. A new boss is one thing, but a new boss with a weird nickname is something else.

I learned many lessons from ET, but one of the most important lessons was to be passionate about whatever you set out to do. No matter the reason for a connection or the expectation of something as routine as a market visit, passion was always embedded in our time together... and I came to expect that.

Effort was not far behind either. ET was driven to be on par with her male counterparts in a male-dominant business, so effort, effervescent effort, was part of how she could offset any disadvantages, real or perceived.

As a leader, ET was far ahead of her time. She played deep within the corporate world dominated by men for twenty years before I met her.

ET was a very emotional leader. At that time, I thought that I understood passion and effort, and perhaps I did in my personal life, like when playing or watching sports, but what I learned from ET was about passion from a professional perspective.

Some would describe ET as more than just emotional or passionate; some would describe her as combative. Let me come back to that word in a moment.

The reality is that ET was effervescent about everything in her life. She was spirited and enthusiastic. That also meant that if ET was on your side, you were enthusiastic about being in her presence. If she was not on your side, you had to hold your own around her, or her passion would steamroll you.

At the end of the day, though, you always knew where you stood with ET, whether you liked it or not. This style turned off many people that worked for her, with her, and even above her. There was a level of intimidation that paired with her style, and I saw many leaders crumble under that level of force.

Now, as I am describing ET, it may sound as though these are negative traits—no, just the opposite.

Back to the word combative and let me add the word conflict. This was not the soft skill stuff that everyone is teaching now. This was in-your-face leadership... but it was a critical component of her success.

Let me share a story that counteracts ET's style but actually highlights why emotion, passion, and conflict have a material place in leadership.

This is a true story, but I will not disclose this person's name due to the nature of our relationship. I never asked to share this story, which is why I will leave this with a level of anonymity.

When discussing leadership styles, being combative or engaging in conflict often gets a bad rap. It is not usually viewed as a positive leadership trait. This is one of the life lessons that will challenge that.

I worked with a senior leader years ago who shared that she had an executive coach prior to taking her current role; she shared with me one evening over dinner what the coach had been working on with her related to her development- managing conflict. In fact, she had multiple coaches from multiple companies for years, helping her with this one developmental area.

This leader had excelled in every place she has operated but had this one persistent issue. She realized that when she led like-minded leaders, she delivered incredible results. However, when she led those who had different styles, particularly those who were willing to engage in debate and pushback, her effectiveness dwindled, and this development area was exposed. One of the examples she shared with me highlighted this deficiency. It centered around having a problematic person on her team to manage.

So, enter the first executive coach. This engagement lasted for about fifteen months. The net result is that she made a little bit of progress but not enough to change the trajectory of this issue. As she moved to a new organization, she was confronted with a similar difficult leader to manage, and this issue again rose to the surface.

So, she engaged with a new executive coach. The second coach was much more curious about the personal life of this leader. As with most things in our life, our issues can trace back to childhood, so the second executive coach went there. Month after month, she met with this leader and probed deeper into her personal life, almost forgetting that there was a professional relationship. The further the executive coach traced back into this leader's life, the more clues relevant to the current challenge they were attempting to solve together began to reveal themselves.

It would have been easy at any point to stop and act upon her assumptions, but the executive coach continued to go deeper. About ten months into the relationship, the executive coach reached a decisive moment, as she described it. As this leader became increasingly uncomfortable with sharing, it only served to create a greater urgency for the executive coach to probe further.

During that session, the conversation shifted from the leader to the leader's parents. For some time, the executive coach believed there had to be a connection but did not want to draw any conclusions. This was that moment to go deeper.

The question ultimately posed by the executive coach was this:

"Tell me about your parent's relationship. How well did they get along?" It would seem like a fairly common question, particularly if you were sitting with a personal counselor; of course, the relationship between this leader and the executive coach was becoming more personal than professional.

With all the executive coach's experience with leaders, even she was unprepared for the answer she received. The answer was, "I never saw my parents argue growing up, never." The leader went on to say, " I truly had no idea what conflict was until it showed up in the workplace. I suppose, as a result, I have been ill-equipped all along to deal with it."

At that moment, this leader realized that she was saying something that this executive coach had never heard- the executive coach's look said it all.

After a very deliberately long and uncomfortable pause, the executive coach responded. She stated the obvious, what her reaction was already saying, "I have never heard that before."

I must admit, I was just as shocked when this leader shared the story with me. My first thought was, as odd as it is, why would anyone lie about that? It actually seemed like an ideal childhood. I mean, who would have ever thought there could be repercussions for being nice?

My second thought was a bit different, though. The word 'sheltered' came to mind.

Sometimes we see something good and believe it is "too good to be true." I do not know if having that cynical view as a default perspective is good. It feels a little judgmental, and at that moment, I might as well have been wearing a black robe. It just did not seem possible. Coming from a household growing up where things were always broken and arguing was an art, I had no conceivable way of relating to this leader's upbringing. It was interesting that this would be the barrier to this leader's success.

All this to say that being combative is not necessarily a bad thing. In addition, being combative can help you solve problems.

Back to ET, being combative was one of her strengths.

With ET, I saw real leadership for the first time in action. I thought I had seen it before in my career but had only seen watered-down versions. People who were willing to stick their necks out a little, but not a lot. People who were willing to make a hard call, but only when they were forced to. People who looked the other way to protect their salary. Perhaps, a bit of the do-just-enough-to-get-by leadership. I am not saying that I had never worked for any good leaders before this point, but ET was different.

I knew that I would gain significant leadership lessons from our relationship, no matter the length of time or the role in which I served. As a result, I became more curious than I had ever been as a leader.

On a personal note, ET had always described herself as a recovering Catholic. Not being of the Catholic religion, I did not quite understand what she meant, but over time it made sense. ET may have claimed to be a Catholic, but she was also openly gay and unapologetic and railed against those who did not accept her for who she was.

I learned much about the Gay and Lesbian community through my connection with ET. My understanding was significantly elevated, primarily due to my long conversations with ET about it. ET always knew at an early age that she was a lesbian and had to stay silent for far too long because of her upbringing and the views imposed upon her. So, when she could break free as an adult, she really broke free.

The most important lesson I learned from ET was about the philosophy of leadership. And it made sense – ET went to college to get a degree in philosophy. However, as she so eloquently shared with me at the beginning of our relationship, no one was hiring philosophers when she graduated college.

ET is also Hudson Institute certified as a coach. No, she was not certified back in the day, but she might as well have been. She had been a master class teacher in leadership for decades... and here I was, getting the lesson for free.

ET was more than a leader – she was a change agent. I do not say that lightly because I believe in the studies proclaiming that only 15% of us are actual change agents; the other 85% are change averse.

ET's role at that time was interesting- she oversaw a large part of the operation, but she was also in charge of diversity at a time when the word diversity scared white men.

Actually, ET scared white men on almost every topic. As an openly gay woman, I could see the body language of other people around her change every time she spoke about it.

Again, ET demonstrated her passion and effort, this time around the topic of diversity. And while she was a gay woman, her passion was not self-serving. Just the opposite – it was about promoting the voice of the voiceless. ET knew she was in a leadership position where she could make a difference.

I believe that one of the reasons that ET and I connected so well from the very beginning is that she is an open-minded person, and she walked the walk. Not because of her lifestyle but because she represented equality and had no issue telling others about it. As I have shared in some of my other writings, there are people who talk about being open-minded until you bring up a subject that causes a response of, "Well, yeah, I am open-minded except for that." I am not saying this to say that being open-minded to everything is the position that everyone should take in their life. All I am saying is do not say that you are open-minded and then find yourself backtracking on almost any topic. This was not ET... and that level of compassion for others and their beliefs was one of ET's most admirable traits.

When it came to business, perhaps no one was better prepared when a new issue arose. Let me put it this way; if we had a Blockbuster debate team, ET would have been the captain. I mean, it did not matter what the subject was; ET seemed to know something about everything, and if you did not come prepared with knowledge, be ready to be schooled.

There is often a debate about whether leadership is taught, or people are born with it. What I will say is this- if you can be born with it, ET was born with it.

One more story on ET. She was an incredible extemporaneous speaker. ET might be the most gifted speaker that I have been around. If not, she was undoubtedly the most gifted extemporaneous speaker. I recall one off-site meeting when we were preparing to host a large group of franchise owners. The size of the meeting and content required our presenters to use a teleprompter. I learned that if you have never used one before, it is difficult to get used to.

So, here we were preparing for this conference, and all the "handlers" were attempting to prepare ET for her presentation. While it was not funny back then, it is certainly funny now.

Seriously, what we were trying to do was not easy. First, we had to slow down the teleprompter; then, we had to speed it up for the next rehearsal. Then she began adlibbing words that were not on the screen. So, after the third or fourth round on site of practicing with the teleprompter, we admitted defeat.

Of course, ET blamed her inability to get traction with her presentation on the teleprompter operator and the person preparing her slides. The moment that the teleprompter disappeared in the final rehearsal, she came to life... she was effervescent. There is no other way to describe it, and at that moment, we realized that we were attempting to have her lead in a way that was not her natural style. What transpired was one of the most inspirational and authentic presentations ever delivered to a group. It was truly magical.

The level of passion that ET demonstrated daily was not normal, particularly in an executive role. However, it does not make it wrong; it actually makes the leader human. As I proceeded throughout my career, emotion did not always play well in key leadership positions, but I recognized the importance of it, nonetheless. Still, where you gain the steadfast hand of a non-emotional, non-reactionary leader, you could lose on the other side related to culture because people do not feel as connected to the non-emotional leader. Unfortunately, that is just what it is.

Even to this day, I consider ET one of the two mentors I could turn to in challenging times for counsel and know that I will walk away with something more than what I went into the conversation with.

After reading all this, you may be wondering – well, what does this level of effervescent effort get you?

Brace yourself for a long answer:

First, it shows that you are a human being. The display of emotion as a leader of people, even though it may be viewed as negative emotion at times, showing up as conflict, still demonstrates that you are highly invested in the work that you do and the people that you do the work with. Showing emotion in the workplace can build trust and establish you as a leader that others want to follow.

The second is authenticity. Showing up as who you are and being open to sharing that with others can also build trust. Authenticity requires transparency. It also requires a high level of engagement and curiosity.

Third, it shows that you care. Back to earlier in the book, when you are conditioned to care, you can never back away from that. Even when you attempt to demonstrate that you do not care, you always come back around to it. It is just who you are. So, for those caring people reading this, I am sure you are nodding your head – you know who you are. It feels like other people have used you, taken advantage of your good nature, most often never returned the favor, etc. That said, I would encourage you to continue to care.

On the other side of this conversation, lack of effort is a choice.

From there, a lack of effort can manifest as a lack of care and, before you know it, you are in the murkiness of indifference. From there, be careful, as mediocrity and indifference could manifest themselves into your everyday life. These manifestations can have grave consequences.

CHAPTER *12*:

The Manifestations

I have discussed many dimensions of mediocrity and indifference in this book.

The fact is this: mediocrity and indifference can, and often do, show up in every facet of our lives. They are unavoidable... even if you successfully eliminate them in the things you can control. Undoubtedly, there will be evidence of mediocrity or indifference throughout your daily journey.

Candidly, it is easier to write about topics like mediocrity and indifference from an academic or philosophical perspective. However, when mediocrity and indifference manifest themselves in real-life situations, it changes everything, and it changed how I decided to talk about these topics in this chapter.

Before I discuss some real-life manifestations, I want to address a couple of abstract ones: hopelessness and depression.

My intention is not to minimize either condition by calling them abstract. I am using abstract in this context because we cannot always see hopelessness and depression due to people masking them. Let me start with hopelessness.

Hopelessness is a condition that draws a direct line to indifference. Hopelessness can make you believe that taking action will not change anything- see the voting conversation earlier in the book.

Hopelessness is a condition that I have severely underestimated. That is until I spent time at the high school of my oldest son, Ryan, years ago. I should have understood hopelessness better, given my upbringing with all the things I longed for but could never have and all the financial hardships I faced. The hard truth is that I began to do better in life and simply forgot what it felt like.

Years ago, I received a request from my son's teacher to come and speak to his class. Of course, I agreed to do it. Ryan was a sophomore in high school, and he thought my job as a regional vice president made me well-suited to take on this opportunity.

Ryan's high school was an average high school. I do not mean that in a negative way. I would describe it as a median high school- if you took all the high schools in the U.S. and ranked them top to bottom, this school would be exactly in the middle: exactly in the middle demographically, exactly in the middle on test scores, and exactly in the middle on household incomes.

As the day drew closer, I prepared many different thoughts to share with this room of students. I also attempted to anticipate what questions would come from this group.

As I talked about my career and the hardships I had gone through to reach and then take advantage of my career opportunities, I could see heads nodding in the room. However, I was perplexed because the overall body language of most of the students was inconsistent with the vibe that I was picking up. Therefore, I did not know what conclusion to draw.

As I finished sharing my story, I had time to take questions from the students. Most of the questions were straight down the middle, with no real surprises. The students seemed satisfied with my responses, but none of my answers were met with a high level of enthusiasm- I was not sure why.

Then one student spoke up. She talked about how going to college was not a reality for her. She also said that she was not optimistic about her future or her ability to have any success. Another student chimed in and said, "I am never going to amount to anything."

I heard the phrase "You are never going to amount to anything" a thousand times growing up. It threw me back to my childhood, and for this discussion, that is not a good thing. This statement would cut right through me as a child, and it is a statement that plagues many households- the declaration by a parent that their child will not be productive or successful... before they even get started in life. Of course, any reasonable person with children would wonder how anybody could or would do that to their child.

Stripping hope away from your own child, especially when there are times when hope is all they have, is just downright cruel.

Back to the classroom. The hopelessness that day in the room was palpable.

I must admit, I was embarrassed that day when I left the school, mostly because I should have known better. I should have been better prepared for that conversation. Perhaps the school ranking, in the middle and not on the bottom, made me believe all was good. Perhaps the balance of race and income levels made this seem like a good school. Perhaps I was just disconnected and living in a bubble. I am going to go with the latter.

I had clearly underestimated hopelessness. I vowed never to do that again.

Hopelessness is an incredibly powerful emotion. So much so that you can describe what success looks like to someone void of hope, you can even give them the door to walk through, but most often, they cannot comprehend it. There is almost a lack of mental acuity even to process it. That is the power of hopelessness.

The manifestation of hopelessness is a lack of confidence, a lack of self-esteem, but maybe most damaging, a lack of belief. Doubt is often waiting at the doorway to come in soon after.

Depression is another manifestation. If anyone were to ask me to define depression, I would describe it this way: Depression is a severe case of a loss of hope.

I recognize that depression is more complicated than that; however, I am drawing a link between hopelessness and depression, just as I am making a connection between mediocrity and indifference. Hopelessness can lead directly to depression, just as indifference can lead directly to mediocrity.

Unfortunately, I have seen depression up close and personal. My wife of 28 years has experienced some form of depression all her life. At times, her depression was literally debilitating. At all times, an uphill battle, a look in the mirror every day asking if it is worth it to continue living. If you have not experienced depression or been close to someone that has, depression is not your run-of-the-mill unhappiness. Often, unhappiness is a moment in time and then things get better.

Depression is on a different plane. People suffering from depression are constantly masking their feelings to avoid being judged by others. However, when their depression is exposed, and they are judged by others, and sometimes harshly, it can begin a vicious cycle of lower self-esteem, lower confidence, more self-doubt, and ultimately a greater level of depression. While masking a problem or condition is not the most productive way to proceed, this option is sometimes the preferred path for the person experiencing depression.

Now, from abstract to reality.

I knew that I could not complete this book without addressing the real-life, present-day application of mediocrity and indifference... and unfortunately, there are examples all around us to choose from.

I positioned many chapters in this book in order for this very reason: saying "I Didn't Know", unfairly comparing, portraying a lack of care, not demonstrating kindness, blaming others, not paying attention to detail, and not giving effort. They all lead to a path that gets us to these manifestations- the feelings actually playing out into behaviors, actions... and consequences.

If you have followed my writings, you know that I love pragmatism and practicality. On that note, something I referenced early in the book, I will come back to again here- the "reasonable person standard."

I provided an example of a "reasonable person standard" response earlier in the book but let me go a little deeper into that example.

The Academy Award-winning actor stepping on the stage to slap a comedic host for telling a joke during the most elegant event of the year shown around the world, arguably the biggest audience of any televised event outside of the Super Bowl, is unreasonable.

It was interesting how everyone interpreted this event and measured the magnitude of it. I found myself in my media room that night, watching the show. My son had friends over at the house that night. A clear sign of the world we live in today- the incident was on social media within seconds. That meant that my son and his friends were aware almost in real-time, although they were not watching the show. Toward the end of the show, we all arrived in the kitchen around the same time for a late-night snack. A conversation about the incident ensued.

One of my son's friends said, "What is the big deal anyway?"

I began to enlighten him and the others who gathered in the kitchen. I used stereotypical terms like "the angry Black man" and "Black-on-Black crime." You can see where I was going with this.

My reflection on this incident with the discussion amongst these young adults was their level of indifference- not in a malicious way, just no emotional attachment to the situation.

I fully accept that I probably overreacted to the situation then and even today, as I will no longer watch movies involving the perpetrator.

However, I firmly believe that my son and his friends grossly underreacted to this situation mainly because they did not identify with the savagery of the moment—the lack of judgment to use any of the other civil options available to remedy the situation. Instead, the nuclear option was chosen.

The relevance here is that I am attempting to inject this "reasonable person standard" again into this chapter to bring logic to the situation and shine the spotlight on mediocrity. You may disagree with it- I am okay with that. I have always said, "In communication, you seek understanding, not agreement." This is an important distinction, as the focus is often on the attempt to move someone to your point of view. This is not that. Ultimately, the Academy Awards situation was a moment in time, but we have all moved on. However, some real-life situations linger...

There are situations where mediocrity and indifference collide, and the worst possible outcome occurs; when the impact is so heinous that you cannot be a bystander; when it is impossible for your heart not to ache; when you cannot avoid engaging in the discussion; when you cannot say "I Didn't Know."

Uvalde.

Unfortunately, I only need to say this one word; you already know what I am talking about. Of course, mostly everyone acknowledged that it was tragic, and they wished that it had not happened, and they sent their thoughts and prayers, and... and... and. You can probably tell by my tone that I am disgusted with the collective response to this tragedy.

Now, some of you will say that it was a mediocre performance by law enforcement, school administrators, city officials, lawmakers, etc. Some of you will say the real issue is not having law enforcement on campus or not having teachers with guns. Some of you will say the problem was the unlocked back door, or propped open door, or jammed door, or locked classroom, or unlocked classroom. Some of you will say that it was a gun issue, some of you will say it was an AR-15 gun issue, or the age of purchase, or lack of universal background checks, or lack of convictions and death penalty sentences for crimes like this. Some of you will blame it on taking prayer out of schools decades ago. Some of you will blame it on immigration. Some of you will blame it on race. Some of you will blame it on former President Barack Obama- he often got blamed for things he could not possibly control, so I had to throw that in. Finally, some of you will blame it on the classroom teachers themselves for, in some way, not protecting the children on that day.

Do you see what I did there? I covered every reason for this tragedy except abortion and climate change... and there is probably someone, somewhere, attempting to make those links too.

This is how complicated every issue in America seems to be these days.

This is why I want what I discuss in this book to matter. For example, in Uvalde, you could see:

A lack of effort, the blame game, people who did not care enough, a lack of attention to detail, and overall, a lot of "I Didn't Know," all on full display.

The number of police and law enforcement officials that stood there doing nothing, only feet from where little children were murdered, is as cowardly of a collective act as I have seen in the history of our country. Yes, I am going in.

The back door unlocked, broken, ajar, left propped open; it does not matter, and yet, that is where many people got stuck in the conversation.

This is Uvalde. 376 police officers and law enforcement officials stood around with their hands in their pockets for seventy-seven minutes.

For those who run to defend the police every time someone criticizes them, all I can say with this tragedy in Uvalde is... be careful.

In the age of technology, we all saw it with our own eyes. The seventy-seven minutes of nothing. It is indisputable, and, as I referenced the term earlier in the book, it is not Fake News.

So, the strategy was to let the kids die, and then we would go in when it was safe. I mean, can you really deduce anything else? Oh yes, there was a lack of a commander. That was the purported reason for inaction. Maybe it was something else; maybe there was something that was missed in our assertion about what happened that day. Perhaps we underestimated an element at play when we ponder what those 376 law enforcement members thought that led to their inaction. Yes, I believe that there was something else at play.

Mediocrity and indifference for sure, and... they were cowards. No, not all, not even most police officers are cowards; however, these police officers lacked courage. Back to an earlier point in the book. Leadership is about meeting the moment. Responding after the fact is not what leadership is about. These officers have trained all their lives for these critical moments. Drill after drill after drill and then the moment arrives, and they shrunk. Not one of them, all of them.

Go ahead, staunch Blue supporters, step on the graves of these ten-year-old children waiting to go to recess, eat their sandwiches at lunch, and then go home and have their little faces kissed and their little bodies hugged by their parents, siblings, and others. How in the world did we get here?

Well, again, mediocrity and indifference amongst 376 police officers and law enforcement officials is how.

Mediocrity and indifference are not some theoretical reveries.

Both are literally playing out before our eyes, and even in the most appalling situations, we somehow manage to rationalize the behavior. There may not be a tragedy in the United States with this many law enforcement and police officers in one place since 9/11. Let that one sit for a moment.

But this is not all about the 376 bystanders. Lawmakers, gunmakers, all levels of elected officials, judges, etc., played a direct or indirect role in this tragedy.

Again, when there is that pit in the back of your stomach, knowing that something can go wrong and there will be nothing you can do about it, we often stand in contemplation afterward. To be fair, no one is a match for an AR-15 assault rifle. But cowardness has no equal, either. The fear of engaging to protect lives appeared to be too high of a risk for this cast of pretend police. As a result, twenty-one people were wiped off the face of the earth forever. How do we just move on?

For these 376 law enforcement members, Uvalde was their defining moment. This was when their courage was needed. But, instead, their cowardness rose to the top. No leadership, no honor, no courage, no respect, no love, no decency, and no action.

To make matters worse, there was a full-scale effort to not let people into the school, including parents willing to die to save their children.

There were many heroic actions on this day- unfortunately, few were performed by law enforcement. A mother was urging the police to enter the building, only to be handcuffed by police. When she was released, she ran into the school, grabbed her kids, and brought them to safety. According to one Texas Department of Public Safety lieutenant interviewed by local news, some officers ran into the school only to grab their children. I cannot confirm that it happened, but I have no reason to believe that he would break "the code" and share this story about his law enforcement brothers if it were not true.

According to the chilling firsthand account of a fourth grader in the room, police officers told children to yell "if you need help." When one little girl did, the gunman immediately shot her.

There is a recent account by a paramedic arriving on the scene. Her recollection of that day was very grim. She arrived and immediately "smelled iron." Yes, it is what you may be thinking it is. There was so much blood at the scene that the paramedic could smell the iron from the blood... before even entering the school. Anyone who has had a severe injury, and lost significant amounts of blood, knows that smell. This is not okay.

A scathing US Justice Department report just released highlighted pleas from terrified 9 and 10-year-old children trapped with the gunman. Cries for help over a 911 call came during the first 37 minutes of the deadly siege. Another 40 minutes would pass before the 18-year-old shooter was killed.

The 575-page report on the botched law enforcement response said, "the victims experienced unimaginable horror and witnessed unspeakable violence as a result of the lack of courage and cascading failures of leadership, decision-making, tactics, policy, and training."

The Critical Incident Review is based on analysis of more than 14,100 documents and more than 260 interviews.

There were five key takeaways from the damning review: Failure to take 'courageous action;' failure to recognize active shooter situation; failure to secure the crime scene; failure to establish standard operating procedures; failure to communicate with families. Basically, law enforcement failed at everything.

I did not need this report to validate everything that I have already written about in this chapter, more than a year ago, but there it is.

At the printing of this book, mass shootings are no longer a unique, isolated event. This is not a narrative about guns, either. Not at all, guns are just instruments. And no, the issue is not the obligatory "mental health" moniker that always gets thrown in allowing for deflection and serving as a monologed transition to the next mass shooting. As I see it, the issue is the presence of mediocrity and indifference.

It is not just that I am angry almost two years after the shooting in Uvalde; I am also sad. I suppose I expect so much more of leaders when leadership is called for.

Two of the children killed in the Uvalde school shooting were decapitated. I know some of you are wondering whether I needed to be that graphic. As usual, someone repeating something gruesome that happened is often held to a higher standard than the person who committed the disgusting act or allowed it to occur. In today's world, it is called "selective outrage."

I am taking the strongest line possible that I can take in print here to get your attention. I don't like what I am writing here perhaps any more than you do reading it, but taking the high road makes sense when you are having a petty argument with your spouse; not when little kids are riddled with bullets.

Let's go a little deeper. The police failed at protecting the school children, but we should not be under the illusion that this is an example of police officers failing at their jobs. What? Yes, as far as we can tell from reports, police at the scene functioned as they usually do, in accordance with standard policing practice. Rather than risk a hail of gunfire to stop the killer, they kept themselves safe.

I am going to the other side of this conversation. Maybe I

am completely wrong here. Using the word coward could be reckless and completely off base. Here is why:

The behavior of the police at Robb Elementary is only shocking if you are committed to a mythic notion of what policing entails. The "thin blue line" does not, as reactionary narratives would have it, separate society from violent chaos. This has never been what police do since the birth of municipal policing.

It is disgusting, but not shocking that police officers would sooner harass and handcuff parents- parents begging them to save their children from a massacre- than run in and put themselves in the line of fire. What is striking, though, is how inconceivable it is to so many people that policing is not what they have been told it is by the police themselves, by those in power, and by the mainstream culture built around those mutually reinforcing myths.

Being a police officer is not among the top ten most dangerous jobs in the U.S.- I know this will strike a nerve with some people. But it just is not. Delivery drivers face more significant risks to their lives at work. I know- this sounds so disrespectful to the police. Well, it is, but only if you believe the myths about policing.

Even the Supreme Court affirmed in 2005 that police departments are not obligated to protect the public. Our safety is quite simply not what our tax dollars, endlessly funneled into glutted police departments, pay for. Meanwhile, two teachers put their bodies in the line of fire and died trying to protect children during the massacre in Uvalde.

I know some of you are shaking your head at this statement- it cannot be true. Here is the evidence: In the case of Town of Castle Rock vs. Gonzales, the Supreme Court ruled that police agencies are not obligated to provide protection of citizens. In other words, police are well within their rights to pick and choose when to intervene to protect the lives and property of others — even when a threat is apparent.

However, there is this. This is the Uvalde Police Department creed:

"The City of Uvalde Police Department serves the community by protecting citizens and property, preventing crime, enforcing laws, and maintaining order. The Uvalde Police Department is committed to provide superior police service to the public in order to protect life, property, and the freedoms provided by the Constitution."

I mean, I did not make this up. I cannot believe that this is still posted on the City of Uvalde Police Department website as of the publishing of this book. On the home page, no less.

The words of the Uvalde Police Department should not be dismissed. Why? Because it is their own words. It is not meant to use their words against them, but remember, kids died. 10-year-old kids died.

Oh also, according to law enforcement doctrine, active shootings require that the first action by officers, no matter their rank, should be to immediately "stop the killing." So, what are we to believe?

I am disgusted about what happened that day in Uvalde in a way that I cannot describe, and I suppose I want you to be too. I will never get over it. I certainly will not get over the mediocrity and indifference that should make it difficult for all involved to sleep at night.

By the way, I am not inferring that this school massacre is more important than any of the other hundreds that have occurred. This one was different because law enforcement was there for the moment, 376 of them, and they still allowed it to happen. That is different.

I recognize that these are heavy topics. But so are mediocrity and indifference. When these conditions go unchecked, the implications are far-reaching.

One more topic to cover in this chapter.

Child sex trafficking. Talk about a topic that no one wants to discuss... which is precisely what perpetrators want. They want us to be so disgusted that we will not engage in the conversation. That then becomes a precursor for the inability to move toward solving the problem.

Again, this is what happens. Something so heinous that, when it is discussed, we are angrier at the person discussing it than we are with the person doing it. I am confident someone will read this and question my integrity of even putting such vile information in my book. And yet, all I am doing is asking us to look closer at those who are committing these crimes... because most of them are your neighbors.

I am not discussing overall human trafficking on a global scale or even human trafficking in the U.S. I am also not discussing sex trafficking on a global or U.S. level. I am drilling down to child sex trafficking, and again, not on a worldwide level, but here in the U.S. specifically.

This is an important distinction because we often want to "boil the ocean" in attempting to solve problems. This global crisis of human trafficking is a daunting task to go after. However, when we focus on what is happening just in the United States, just with sex trafficking and just with children in particular, we can begin to see the problem more clearly and move to solutions.

What exactly is child sex trafficking?

Child sex trafficking is where children and young people are tricked, forced, or persuaded to leave their homes and are moved or transported for the purpose of being sexually exploited.

Children trafficked for sexual exploitation are at high risk of prolonged periods of sexual violence, physical injuries, sexually transmitted infections, and, for girls, multiple pregnancies.

I must go here: Imagine your 14-year-old daughter, who may spend an unreasonable amount of time on social media, making videos and gathering friends and likes, gets excited about the interest people are paying her. Ultimately, it leads to getting dropped off at the local mall or coffee shop to meet someone new, who then abducts her, and within 24 hours, she is somewhere halfway around the world being sold for sexual favors, and you have no context of how to find out where she may be. Can you imagine that? Well, it is happening every day here in the United States.

On average, a child enters the U.S. sex trade at 12 to 14 years old. Many are runaway girls who were sexually abused as children.

Most of the time, victims are trafficked by someone they know, such as a friend, family member, or romantic partner. I am begging you not to gloss over this. I want you to take a moment to think about all the people who have access to your children through school, church, sports, and other extracurricular activities... or who happen to live next door.

Okay, let me push on.

Predators can rent a child for a single sex act for an average of $90. Often, that child is forced to have sex twenty times per day, six days a week.

Trafficking usually occurs in hotels, motels, online websites, and at truck stops in the U.S.

According to the Federal Human Trafficking Report, in 2018, over half (51.6%) of the criminal human trafficking cases active in the U.S. were sex trafficking cases involving children.

This is disgusting, I know. But so is indifference- **the ethical and moral ability to look away, do nothing... and be okay with it.**

Many of you may say that this child sex trafficking issue is a border issue. No doubt, there is an element at the border that must be addressed. But again, I am attempting to get us to focus here. Studies estimate that 83% of child trafficking victims in the U.S. are American children... trafficked by Americans. It is always easier when we can deflect the responsibility to someone else. In this case, we are the someone else.

In the U.S., child sex trafficking is aggravated by three key factors: predatory social media use, pornography, and broken families.

Social media platforms provide market access for traffickers and pedophiles in the United States. These men first meet and groom minors for sexual encounters over social media, often posing as boyfriends. Once they have lured their victims in, they use social media to advertise and sell the minors for sex.

One organization, United Against Human Trafficking, estimates that "fifty-five percent of victims of U.S. child sex trafficking aged 7 to 11 are recruited through social media apps and websites... Because of this, fewer than ten percent of cases happen by kidnapping."

How many alarming statistics can I provide to you at one time? Age 7? You might want to check that tablet or cell phone that you gave your second grader to keep them busy so that they don't bother you. This is a new day and the bad guys are different. They dress and look like all of us, but are more sinister than ever before. You know what is sinister? A middle-aged, well-dressed woman posing as a concerned mother and luring young girls and boys into vehicles, allegedly to take them home. Instead, they are taken to a location and immediately forced into sex trafficking.

There is a passive nature that is the raw definition of mediocrity. This casual "it could never happen to my child" mentality is what almost caused our democracy to fall a few years ago. I mean, there was no way Americans would ever storm our own Capitol building, right? What I want you to revisit is the number of lies, insults, threats, commands, and devisive acts that were collectively overlooked for years that led to that moment. Mediocrity and indifference. It did not have to happen... and neither does child sex trafficking.

Second, child sex traffickers also frequently use minors to produce pornography. This creates a double harm: Not only are children sexually abused, but videos of their abuse are uploaded to major pornography websites, and their abuse is played repeatedly.

Third, the most vulnerable children in the United States are those raised in single-parent homes, especially if an unrelated male is present. Children are eleven times more likely to suffer sexual and physical abuse in such situations. Women with daughters must be extra careful about dating a new man. For the sake of your child, pay attention. If the new boyfriend wants to babysit your daughter while you go to work, consider that a red flag. Yes, in this instance, I am proposing a guilty-until-proven-innocent mentality. Also, without the protection of a mother and father in the home, children are more likely to run away, go missing, or spend time in the foster care system. In 2016, the National Center for Missing and Exploited Children found that 86% of child sex trafficking victims were in the care of social services when they went missing. Talk about a broken system.

Child sex trafficking is everywhere. It is easy to find if you know where to look. For example, an exit off an interstate highway with a truck stop, an Asian massage parlor, or an adult superstore. Each of these locations separately is statistically more likely to be a location for trafficking, including the interstate itself. If they are grouped together, the statistical possibilities increase dramatically.

Knowing the signs of trafficking can help give a voice to children. Sometimes children will not understand that what is happening to them is wrong. Or they might be scared to speak out.

It may not be evident that a child has been sex trafficked, but you may notice unusual or unexpected things. They might:

- spend a lot of time doing household chores.
- rarely leave their house or have no time for playing.
- be orphaned or living apart from their family.
- live in low-standard accommodations.
- be unsure which country, city, or town they are in.
- be reluctant to share personal information or where they live.
- not be registered with a school.
- have money or things you would not expect them to have.
- not understand what has happened to them is abuse- especially if they have been groomed.
- believe they are in a relationship with their abuser and unaware they are being exploited.
- think they played a part in their abuse or have broken the law.
- feel very guilty or ashamed about the abuse they have suffered.

This is that moment of truth. Pay attention to details around you. Become more vigilant about your surroundings. Look out for kids in your family and in your neighborhood, like many parents did in the more innocent generations of our country.

Child sex trafficking is so invisible in our communities that we are not compelled to action. Do not allow indifference to creep in here. Do not avoid the topic. Your engagement may save lives and save families.

Let me bring this back to the top level about mediocrity and indifference.

I worked with an employee at Starbucks years ago, who uttered this statement, "The current state of racism in our country is almost like humidity at times. You cannot see it, but you can feel it."

She made this statement in a group discussion about race relations at the Starbucks headquarters in December 2014.

So too is true of the current state of mediocrity and indifference... until it manifests itself in real-life, present-day situations.

I am making this statement in 2024 about mediocrity and indifference. Not in concept, not in theory. Instead, because the smell of iron in the air from gallons of blood lost or a child's head lying on the ground should compel you to action. Even babies are being sex trafficked. Infants. I am not going to unpack that here. I believe you have heard enough.

I must do this. I need you to be shaken. To be outraged. To be mad enough to do something. Be mad at me. I am willing to take this on the chin if it will save your children or grandchildren from future harm, either from school shootings or sex trafficking.

What I am describing is mediocrity and indifference at their worst. This is a combination that is so dangerous that it can end civilizations.

Do my remarks seem melodramatic? If your answer is yes, I will direct you to ask the people of Ukraine how they felt about the possible risk of the end of their civilization just two short years ago. We should never take the posture of 'things are impossible and could never happen to us.' Invariably, that is often when things do happen. I suppose you could make the case that we are always at the crossroads, but the one facing us now has a different level of complexity. Again, people from past generations will say that they went through more significant challenges. That could be true but consider the alternative- it may not be true. We may be closer to the edge than we believe, and thus be on the precipice of the most treacherous time in history.

This is where I come back to hope and possibilities.

There are plenty of people with no hope for success in their life. Life has simply beaten them down and turning that around will not be easy.

There are people with incredible hope but no power to make substantial changes or the means to achieve their dreams.

Some have the power but have lost hope. However, with the

right circumstances, this group could again begin to feel like their influence can make a difference.

There are even some who have the power and the hope but choose the "lighter" and "safer" topics to focus on, like Save The Whales. Yes, I love whales, but do you know what I love even more? 10-year-old little kids making it home safely every day. Not just in stopping school shootings but in addressing the real underbelly of our society- things like child sex trafficking.

Perhaps, the worst combination of all in our society are those who have the power but do not care enough to do for the common good of others- either those in charge of companies, those who are elected, those who are the wealthiest 1%, or worst, those who fit in all three categories. This is where danger lives. The next step with this group is misuse of their power. It begins with white-collar crimes but can end with reckless behavior that puts civilizations at risk.

Manifestations are not all bad. We see heroic stories of people who decided to step forward and positively impact someone else's life. However, if I tell feel-good stories about manifestations, we smile and keep moving forward in our daily lives. This is that moment to stop, address mediocrity, eliminate indifference, and engage.

As I referenced in the beginning of the book, justice, peace, kindness, joy, and happiness are under attack every day, primarily because of rampant mediocrity and indifference. I implore you to join the fight for good.

Let me exhale here and attempt to put all of this together.

CHAPTER 13:

Putting It All Together

Mediocrity and indifference are literally a referendum on how you live your life.

Not caring or not giving your total effort to any part of your life is a recipe for massive regrets later.

So, how do you avoid living a life of mediocrity?

Broadly, I would say to replace mediocrity with excellence. I know- I owe you something a little more specific than that.

Well, first, strive for perfection. Those who say you should not strive for perfection are often leading a mediocre life... I am just calling it as I see it. Striving for perfection does not mean being perfect either... deep down inside, even the striving perfectionists know that. It simply means that your starting goal is 100%, but you may ultimately achieve an 80-85% result. That is vastly different than starting with an 80% expectation of success and allowing a 60-65% result to be your standard. The latter sounds a lot like mediocrity.

Avoiding mediocrity also means taking the time to perfect your craft, whatever that craft is. And no, practice does not make you perfect, but practice does make you better. I know that is an opinion, but it happens to be the opinion of most people who put in practice time and got better.

If you have even a seed of doubt about this, try pole vaulting for the first time. My advice, bring lots of first aid supplies. That said, I am confident that a few months of practice will generate progress that will show improvement from your starting point.

This is also true of leadership. For example, taking the extra time to provide performance feedback, that additional review of financials, or extra preparation for a market visit will sharpen your leadership skills. Leadership takes practice, no different than any other developing skill.

Part of avoiding a life of mediocrity is to avoid mediocrity. This is not meant to be wordplay. It simply means taking action to change your course. You know what you must do when you feel like you are not giving something your all.

The satisfaction of giving something all your effort should be rewarding, no matter what the results. Also, do not let others around you turn the word perfection into a bad word. Unmotivated people will tantalize you with this word to make you feel that your standards are too high, and you should "come down here with the rest of us." Giving in and falling back is tempting, but this is potentially a step toward mediocrity.

Second, allow yourself to be okay with imperfection. I know this sounds like a contradiction to the first point. But it is not, and I will explain.

We are all beset with imperfections. Too much focus on those imperfections can drain your confidence and self-esteem. Accepting those imperfections can liberate you from pursuing perfection and allow you to step back and assess your overall development as a person... and potentially as a leader of others.

Attempting to be perfect, as with any strength overleveraged, can become a weakness.

I have learned a valuable life lesson from my children. They have collectively told me they want to see me make mistakes, have an off day. But not with negative intention.

When my children shared this with me, I honestly did not know how to react to the comment. Admittedly, there was a bit of defensiveness on my part. I mean, I am attempting to live a life of looking at the positive and being a role model for them and others, so why in the world would I settle for less than greatness?

It became clear that my quest for greatness inadvertently upped the ante for each of my children. This was true of them going to college, even though I did not pressure them to do so, or so

I thought. In reflection, sharing or even reminding them that I had set aside money in a 529 Plan to go to college can be construed as more than a subtle nudge that they should go to college. I am confident that I never told any of my three children that they must go to college, but I am convinced that is what they heard. This is why parenting does not come with a manual or at least a manual that can truly capture the real-life challenges of raising another human being.

More directly, to my earlier point, I went through a period a couple of years back when I would send a daily text to the family group chat. I would typically send a motivational message meant to inspire everyone in the family to have a wonderful day. However, on occasion, the opposite occurred. At times, my overblown optimism was met with resistance and some skepticism. It would have been easier to digest this criticism had it come from outside the family unit. Instead, it came from within- the words sabotage and betrayal came to mind, but I recognized those were too strong of word choices to describe this situation.

This is why inspiring someone else is tricky- what is effective for one person is not the same for someone else... and you must be okay with that, especially as a leader.

In my most recent day job, I rebooted and began sending out an inspirational quote of the day. I have been doing this daily for almost three years, including weekends and holidays. In part because the businesses I lead are open every day, and therefore, someone in our company is working every day. More importantly, though, on the human side, our life problems do not take a day off.

This inspirational message was sent to hundreds of leaders every day, and I can say that almost every day over the past three years, two or three people have hit reply and responded to the message of the day. Most often, it is that the message was just what they needed to take on the day, more specifically, that day. Sometimes, it is just a simple thank you. Of course, that was not lost on me; we had been in the middle of a pandemic- that was enough of a catalyst for me to begin the daily affirmations. I felt like people needed inspiration more than ever before.

When inspiration is absent, a leadership gap can open the door for mediocrity and indifference to come in and trip us up. This can lead us to moments of apathy in which we question why we are doing what we are doing, which can lead us to convince ourselves that what we are doing does not matter. Did you see how quickly I got there?

So, avoiding mediocrity is about more than striving for perfection. Creating balance and allowing for imperfections is not just acceptable; it is necessary. Honestly, setting unrealistic expectations can send you into a tailspin and land you in the space of mediocrity, so be careful.

As for my children, I learned a valuable lesson about vulnerability. The more I showed up as a flawed human being, the more they were willing to show their flaws. Life just works that way.

Third, give yourself a break. I often hear people say that they are their own worst critics. I have done a lot of thinking about this statement over the years. In conclusion, I am unsure if it is a good or bad thing. Here is why:

On the one hand, we may not be critical enough of ourselves, and if we are our own worst critic, in this situation, we will leave potential improvement or achievement on the table. I am not saying that anyone intentionally sets a low bar for themselves- that would be unfair to make that assertion. I am saying that life usually teaches us that letting in outside information is a good thing for personal growth... even when it is not agreeable to us. That said, if you are comfortable with the level of criticism you levy upon yourself, then so be it. Just make sure it is enough to stand up to outside scrutiny or be able to defend against it.

Let's explore the other side of this- you are so critical of yourself that you erode your self-confidence and self-esteem by setting unrealistic expectations, but more importantly, not being able to pick yourself up when you do not achieve the self-imposed goal.

However, there is an upside here. Being your own worst critic will help you avoid a life of mediocrity simply because you are pointed towards something. Purpose is in place, enabling you to create action to avoid mediocrity.

No matter what your lot in life is, giving yourself a break does not mean you gave up on your goals or are not achieving them; it is simply what it says.

The hard truth is that no one can do that for you. Now, others around you may notice that you need a mental or physical break. Good for you if you have those people in your life. Self-awareness and self-regulation are still vital, as others around you should serve as a good backup plan, not a driver of your destiny.

Finally, gain alignment on what success looks like. Easy to say but often challenging to do. However, the irony is not taking time to do this is actually the common pitfall. How often do you sit in a dark, quiet room and think about what you would consider success to be in your personal life? Again, this is an area in which no one else can give you the answer.

On a professional level, it is not so different. It may require more collaboration with others, but stopping to define success is critical... and that is not even the finish line as you must make it measurable and track it and check and adjust along the way. Taking the time upfront to put a stake in the ground will increase your chance of success.

Success is often viewed as a moving target- hard to define and different depending on the situation. If true, we all know how difficult it can be to hit a moving target.

Let me pivot now and talk about indifference. So, how do you avoid living a life of indifference?

Well, the answers are not that different from the answers about mediocrity, at least in principle. You must remember that indifference is not about what you do but how you feel. You must ask yourself if you have a burning desire for the things you are doing. If not, indifference has crept in, at least to some level.

Broadly here, I would say you must replace indifference with intentionality.

First, be intentional about spending time on things you are passionate about. It may even be something you believe you will be passionate about that you have not done yet.

Passion is an emotion, so, in some respect, it could be just as challenging to assess as the abstract aspect of indifference. And yet, if I told you that your favorite musical artist was going on tour and I had two free front-row tickets... well, I do not have to say much more about that. You can literally feel what goes on in your body when presented with what I just described... and you would arrive an hour early, as I referenced in the preface of the book. That is passion.

When it comes to anything you love to do- playing tennis, crocheting, cooking; if you are excited when you do it and when you are finished, you cannot wait until you can do it again, that is passion.

Passion is rarely overused. Yes, I suppose that passion could tip over into obsession, but I am on a positive vibe here. As I referenced in an earlier chapter, do not let an underachiever call you a perfectionist, and do not let indifferent people call you obsessive just because your passion for something is greater than theirs.

Not often discussed as a critical factor in passion is anticipation. Anticipation can lead to purpose, and now your life has meaning-you care more, and the circle begins again. See how quickly I got there again? It can happen on something positive, like passion, just like it did on something negative, like a lack of inspiration.

Having something to look forward to is immensely powerful. Do not underestimate that.

Second, purpose is different from passion. Both have been well packaged in statements like 'living a purpose-driven life'... or have they?

Not exactly. Here is where the alignment between purpose and passion falls apart.

In fact, I would submit that purpose helps more with eliminating mediocrity, and passion is more of a catalyst for eliminating indifference. So, another way of describing this is: Purpose is the work; passion is the joy.

I have friends who are car enthusiasts. I happen to be a car enthusiast as well. However, where my friends and I break apart on this subject is that most of them get geeked out over the size of the engine, the torque, and horsepower, even the turning radius- the mechanics of the car. What excites me about a car is driving it. I am somewhat interested in cylinders, as I have had a V12 car; however, the handling of the car while driving it was what got me excited- that is passion. By the way, when I would drive my V12 car, others often educated me about it; of course, everyone wanted to race me. I never really understood it. All I knew was that I had two V6 engines side by side under my hood, wrapped in such a way that the engine was called a W12, and when I stepped on the gas, it was an unfair fight with others who wanted to race. I refrained... well, most of the time.

Do not get me wrong; purpose is important. However, purpose is the functional and mechanical part of getting the work done. Passion is getting the functional and mechanical work done... but led by emotion.

Passion is hard to define, but you know it when you see it. Let me give you an example in my own life.

From the time I first watched basketball on television- I mean, once the NBA Finals were no longer on tape delay. You might have to look this one up. It was the most ridiculous thing at the time, but it was for real. You will be shocked when you learn more about tape delay. Okay, I will tell you. Tape delay is the practice of intentionally delaying a radio and television broadcast of live material to air at a later time. Often, it was done simply out of a lack of interest by viewership to make it available in real-time. I know; it seems like a ridiculous idea now.

It was 1979, and I watched the college basketball tournament for the first time. It was a game featuring Magic Johnson from

Michigan State and Larry Bird from Indiana State. It was indeed the rebirth of the National Basketball Association. Yes, I know that is a bit confusing because it was a college basketball game, but the attention on that game, starring Magic Johnson and Larry Bird, elevated the focus on the NBA draft the following season. Before you knew it, Magic and Bird were facing off as hated rivals for the Lakers and Celtics, respectively... the NBA was back.

This moment in time developed my passion for basketball. I had such a passion for playing basketball that I would play every day, and I do mean every day. This includes the days in middle school when I was forbidden to play basketball after school. I took a few beatings from staying after school to play basketball. No, I do not mean that in a figurative sense; I mean literal beatings. But it was okay- it was totally worth it. That is how much I loved basketball. Yes, this was when corporal punishment was apparently legal. I fully understand the dramatic nature in which I am using the term corporal punishment, but there is no other way to describe it. I took the beatings, though, every time, and by the next day, I had already forgotten about it, so I would do it all over again.

The point of this story is that this is what passion looks like. An indifferent reaction would have led to me say it was not worth it. But, in retrospect, playing basketball every day was worth the beatings. Seriously.

Finally, do not allow others to mute your passion. Said differently, do not allow people to drag you down to their level of indifference. If there is something that you feel strongly about, stay feeling strongly about it. You developed that passion based on a life experience or a strong curiosity to try something new.

If you are going to be indifferent towards people or situations in your life, I hope it is on something ridiculously small, like not picking up the balled-up piece of paper you missed the trash can with. Do not let indifference leave you second-guessing your decisions and, on a bigger scale, your life. The great news is that every day is a chance for a new start. The day may still not go as well as the day before, but guess what? We then get to try it again... and again.

Similarly, do not let indifference strip you of passion. The last time I checked, we only have one life to live unless you know something I do not know... or if you believe in reincarnation. Reincarnation? I suppose I have time for one more digression...

I watched a movie called 'The Reincarnation Of Peter Proud' when I was ten years old. As I learned afterward, the movie was not appropriate for a ten-year-old. Not for the reasons you may be thinking- there was no nudity or profanity. It was that it was a troubling topic to digest at the age of ten. After watching that movie, I believed reincarnation was real and would not be convinced to believe otherwise. Outside of the fear of what I had seen, I was still a little boy, so I began wondering what animal I would return as and when. I was convinced that I was already reincarnated, so I built every contraption that might enable time travel so that I could go to the location of my prior reincarnated entity and sort all this out.

Since that time, I have done what every other adult would do- I rewatched the movie! I was able to find a used version online and bought it. You can probably guess the outcome- I was not scared and no longer believed in reincarnation.

Let me put a final bow on all of this.

I know this all sounds easy- stop comparing, care more, work to overachieve, pay attention to detail, give maximum effort, spread kindness, stop blaming others, go the extra mile, and work on removing hopelessness and depression.

I wish it were that easy, but it is not.

Mediocrity and indifference are all around us and sometimes within us. So, it requires a conscious effort at times to fight through and stay focused on improvement and not let the cynicism of the world take away your ability to care deeply- the caring so deeply that you act when action is needed on those things that pull on your moral and ethical heartstrings... instead of looking away.

It is okay to hold other people accountable too. In fact, I believe we have a moral obligation to do so.

Replacing mediocrity with excellence and replacing indifference with intentionality will yield huge benefits in your personal and professional life.

Now, go save the world that needs to be saved.